Vintage Postcards for the Holidays

Identification & Value Guide

Robert & Claudette Reed

COLLECTOR BOOKS

A Division of Schroeder Publishing Co., Inc.

Cover design by Beth Summers
Book design by Mary Ann Hudson

COLLECTOR BOOKS
P.O. Box 3009
Paducah, Kentucky 42002-3009
www.collectorbooks.com

PRINTED IN GERMANY.

Copyright © 2002
Robert & Claudette Reed

The current values in this book should be used only as a guide. They are not intended to set prices, which vary from one section of the country to another. Auction prices as well as dealer prices vary greatly and are affected by condition as well as demand. Neither the authors nor the publisher assumes responsibility for any losses that might be incurred as a result of consulting this guide.

Searching For A Publisher?

We are always looking for people knowledgeable within their fields. If you feel that there is a real need for a book on your collectible subject and have a large comprehensive collection, contact Collector Books.

Contents

Liberty and Justice For All

Our country stands for Humanity
And may we be Loyal and True
To the flag that ever protects us—
Old Glory, the red, white and blue.

Robert and Claudette Reed have produced several books on antiques and collectibles over the years with particular focus on advertising and paper collectibles. Together they operate Antique and Collectibles News Service which provides illustrated articles to publications in the United States, Canada, and Australia. They reside in Knightstown, Indiana.

Introduction

There were, of course, holidays in America and the rest of the world long before postcards were in vogue. And the celebration of certain holidays continued long after the golden age of such postcards had ceased.

In historic terms, kinship between favored holidays and the American postcard was relatively short lived. Greeting postcards, paying tribute to holidays as widely accepted as Christmas and as narrowly noted as birthdays, were in general use for about 30 years from the early twentieth century until the onset of the Great Depression of the 1930s. Of that time, historians generally consider the period from roughly 1906 to around 1917 as the "golden era" of holiday postcards.

Postcards with their brilliant printing and standard size arrived at a time when other greeting cards were often frilly and too bulky for mailing. Before the postcard, an envelope (often as expensive, if not more expensive, than the greeting cards themselves) was necessary for mailing.

Greeting postcards were less restrictive. The subject matter could vary and the artwork could be dazzling, just as long as the image fit the standard format of the single card. The results were striking. Some were even considered art.

In England the renowned publisher Raphael Tuck said in the early 1900s that competition for future postcard designs would be directed at "fostering the love of art and encouraging the collecting of artistic postcards." At one point a major magazine of the time observed that the collecting of postcards early in the twentieth century had risen "to the level of collecting works of art."

Certainly some very talented artists, including Ellen Clapsaddle, H.B. Griggs, Frances Brundage, and Mary Evans Price (later of Fisher-Price toys fame), all contributed their fine efforts to holiday postcards. So did a host of other artists. Long after the British had turned to other forms of printed greetings, the holiday postcard was still immensely popular in America. Literally millions were printed and distributed during the first dozen or so years of the "new" twentieth century.

Now, nearly a century later, postcards are being reconsidered. New Year's, Valentine's Day, St. Patrick's Day, Easter, Halloween, Thanksgiving, Christmas, and other postcards remain unique artwork in a vintage frame.

Congratulations, posted 1911, $5.00 – 6.00.

Santa on New Year greeting, 1909, Tuck, $12.00 – 15.00.

New Year's Day

Girl with sheep crook, posted 1904, $3.00 – 5.00.

As fate would have it, holiday greeting postcards came along in the United States about the same time it was really fashionable to celebrate the new year with a bang.

Citizens of late nineteenth century America were known to blow a whistle, ring a bell, and perhaps even bang a drum or two to mark the festive event. It was also a time when such images as the New Year's Baby and the bearded Father Time with his familiar scythe began to be seen. Naturally all of these things were used to illustrate colorful postcards.

By the very early 1900s New Year's Day already had a long history going for it. Some experts in fact considered it to be the world's oldest holiday with recorded festivals dating back to the days of ancient Babylonia. The Egyptians, meanwhile, were said to have divided the year into twelve months of thirty days each. Since they were using a calendar of 365 days there was an extra five days at the end of the year which they sort of divined as a party time. Since the party days actually belonged to no month they were to be spent celebrating the coming of Sothis.

In Egypt on New Year's eve the pharaoh was called upon to rededicate the temples of the country. Assisting him were the queen and various high priests. The following day, New Year's Day, marked the height of the celebration. Later the Romans also celebrated the holiday and called it Kalends. For a time the event was changed to March 1 but by 153 B.C. it was officially made January 1 for the entire Roman empire.

It was said that the Romans had a greeting for the celebration: *Anno novo faustum felix tibi sit.* Roughly translated it meant "may the New Year be happy and lucky for you." Besides the greeting, the Romans also liked to present green branches known as strenae as a gift on that special occasion. At times they were also used to decorate doorways to mark the event. The branches were apparently named for the Roman goddess of health, Strenia, and were said to be symbols of health and vitality.

Children and clock, posted 1905, $5.00 – 6.00.

Later the custom spread to Mediterranean countries where branches of laurel (a form of the popular cooking ingredient bay leaf) were presented with equal pride and well wishing. Various ivy, holly, and fir branches also came to be used. And at times the branches became wreaths or garlands. Druids were said to have celebrated the new year with branches of mistletoe, which they believed to be a sacred plant. The mistletoe branches were presented to friends in hopes of blessings for the coming year.

At some point during the Middle Ages, New Year's Day varied for some reason, say historians, between January 1 and January 6. But for the most part January 1 prevailed and endured. Even as early as the fifteenth century Europeans were known to craft and decorate a type of New Year celebration cards.

Year Date, 1906, $5.00 – 6.00.

Thus the holiday was well established in the culture when Americans discovered postcards as a means of further wishing friends and relatives a traditional happy New Year. Actually they became some of the very first holiday greeting postcards to be put in use, with many of them predating 1907.

Besides the New Year's Baby (which was already a standard in the Tournament of Roses parade in California) and Father Time, there was a wealth of other images on those nifty greeting postcards including clovers, traditional branches of greenery, swastikas, coins, horseshoes, and pigs. At the time, in the early 1900s, pigs were consider a major symbol of good luck. Moreover there was an abundance of time-signifying candles and calendars, along with a variety of clocks. There were also New Year's cards featuring children, cats, mushrooms, and sometimes even Santa wishing the holiday postcard receiver a happy New Year.

Besides all the appealing illustrations of the standard New Year postcard, there were also year date cards. These postcards featured a specific year such as 1908 or 1909 prominently on the front and were therefore good for only a single year.

Like so many other holiday postcards, New Year's holiday postcards were issued in great numbers starting with the early 1900s and continuing to around 1913. After that date, they sharply declined in number, although they were still available to a degree in the 1920s and even beyond.

Besides being a salute to the first holiday of the year, such postcards were often the only means of sharing information within the ever-growing family circle. An intimate look at life on the very last day of 1912 was provided in this hand-written message on the back of one particular New Year's Day card:

Your postcard received. We had our dinner yesterday. Roys did not get here. They are all sick. We are all fairly well and got our Butchering done. I am glad of it. The Cholera is pretty bad around here. We had a big rain last night and the snow is about all gone. Best wishes to you all for a Happy New Year. Aunt Ella.

Girl with basket, $6.00 – 7.00.

Clock and pig, $4.00 – 5.00.

Flowers, design, posted 1907, $2.00 – 3.00.

Horseshoe, posted 1908, $5.00 – 6.00.

Calendar, posted 1908, $3.00 – 4.00.

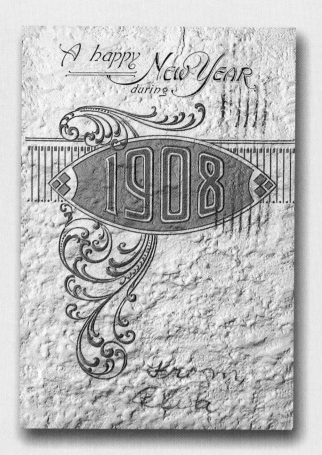

Year Date, 1908, $6.00 – 8.00.

Man outside inn, International Art Pub, $5.00 – 6.00.

Little girl, posted 1909, $6.00 – 7.00.

Village scene, $4.00 – 5.00.

Wreath, fold-down flap, $7.00 – 8.00.

Flowered horseshoe, posted 1909,
$2.00 – 3.00.

Boy, four-leaf clovers, posted 1909,
$6.00 – 8.00.

Colonial couple, $5.00 – 6.00.

Horseshoe, flowers, posted 1909,
$5.00 – 6.00.

Messenger boy in uniform, posted 1909,
$15.00 – 18.00.

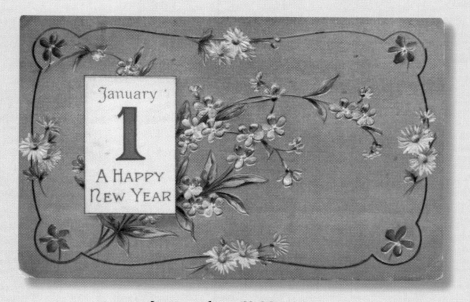

January date, $3.00 – 4.00.

Candle, church, posted 1909, $8.00 – 10.00.

Birds, church, $5.00 – 6.00.

Snow scene, $3.00 – 4.00.

Year Date, 1909, with airship,
$15.00 – 18.00.

Three elves, posted 1909, $6.00 – 8.00.

Year Date, 1909, $5.00 – 6.00.

Bell, posted 1909, $5.00 – 6.00.

Year Date, 1909, $5.00 – 6.00.

Snow scene, posted 1910, $4.00 – 5.00.

Woman with tray, posted 1909,
$10.00 – 12.00.

Boy, horseshoe, posted 1910,
$6.00 – 8.00.

Village scene, $4.00 – 5.00.

Wishbone, flowers, dated 1910,
$5.00 – 6.00.

Girl with bonnet, posted 1910,
$8.00 – 10.00.

Snow scene, $3.00 – 4.00.

Children, basket, posted 1910, $8.00 – 10.00.

Church scene, $3.00 – 4.00.

Bells, holly, $3.00 – 4.00.

January date, $2.00 – 3.00.

Silver bells, posted 1911, $2.00 – 3.00.

Horseshoe, posted 1911, $3.00 – 4.00.

House, snow, posted 1911,
$2.00 – 3.00.

Flower, $2.00 – 3.00.

MY NEW YEARS WISHES
I WISH YOU FRIENDS
I WISH YOU HEALTH
I WISH YOU COMFORT
I WISH YOU WEALTH

Star, snow scene, $2.00 – 3.00.

Holly, posted 1911, $2.00 – 3.00.

Stringed instrument, posted 1911,
$2.00 – 3.00.

Two horseshoes, posted 1911, $3.00 – 4.00.

Three babies at fence,
$4.00 – 5.00.

Woman, flowers, posted
1911, $2.00 – 3.00.

Church, snow scene,
$3.00 – 4.00.

Holly, posted 1911, $2.00 – 3.00.

Holly, snow scene, posted 1911,
$3.00 – 4.00.

Clock, snow scene, $2.00 – 3.00.

Winged figure, moon, $8.00 – 10.00.

Holly, posted 1912, $2.00 – 3.00.

Holly, posted 1911, $2.00 – 3.00.

Clover, horseshoe, $3.00 – 4.00.

U.S. Capitol, posted 1913, $7.00 – 8.00.

Children, umbrella, $3.00 – 4.00.

Small scene, posted 1912, $3.00 – 4.00.

Flowers, scene, posted 1912, $2.00 – 3.00.

Ice skating, $2.00 – 3.00.

Delicate flowers, pig, dated 1912,
$4.00 – 5.00.

Bird, scene, posted 1913, $3.00 – 4.00.

Church, posted 1913, $2.00 – 3.00.

Prosperous banner, posted 1912,
$3.00 – 4.00.

Little girl, basket, 1914, $8.00 – 10.00.

Happy New Year, 1912, $3.00 – 4.00.

Church, wishbone, $3.00 – 4.00.

Clock, flower, 1914, $3.00 – 4.00.

Small calendar, posted 1914, $2.00 – 3.00.

Horseshoe, clover, $3.00 – 4.00.

Clock, posted 1915, $2.00 – 3.00.

Flowers, scene, posted 1914, $2.00 – 3.00.

Holly, posted 1915, $2.00 – 3.00.

Child in swing, $4.00 – 5.00.

Birds, bells, $3.00 – 4.00.

Flowers, horseshoes, $3.00 – 4.00.

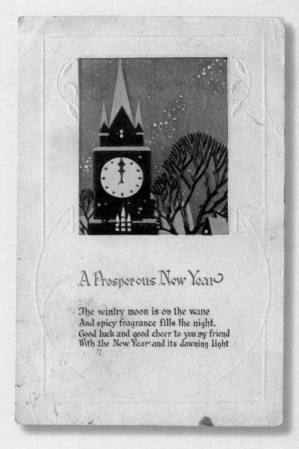

Church, $2.00 – 3.00.

Father Time, automobile, 1916, $18.00 – 22.00.

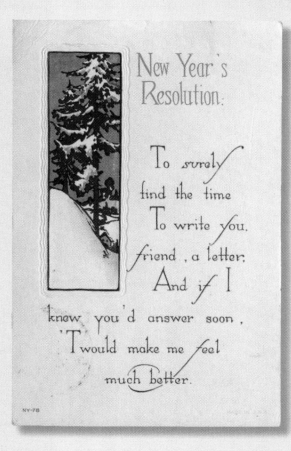

New Year's
Resolution:

To surely
find the time
To write you,
friend, a letter.
And if I

knew you'd answer soon,
'Twould make me feel
much better.

Snow scene, posted 1917, $2.00 – 3.00.

New Year Greetings.

May New Year single you out
• • • for a blessing,
And double the joy you're
• • • • • • at present possessing.

Winter scene, posted 1917, $2.00 – 3.00.

A
Happy New Year

Two birds, $3.00 – 4.00.

Clock, stream, posted 1917, $3.00 – 4.00.

Ornate flowers, $2.00 – 3.00.

A HAPPY NEW YEAR.

OF ALL GOOD THINGS THIS SEASON,
TO-DAY I CHOOSE BUT TWO
THE BLUEBIRD FOR HAPPINESS
AND HAPPINESS FOR YOU.

Birds in flight, posted 1918, $3.00 – 5.00.

Well dressed couple,
$3.00 – 5.00.

House, snow, posted 1919,
$2.00 – 3.00.

Windmill, $2.00 – 3.00.

Bells, $2.00 – 3.00.

Romantic couple, $4.00 – 5.00.

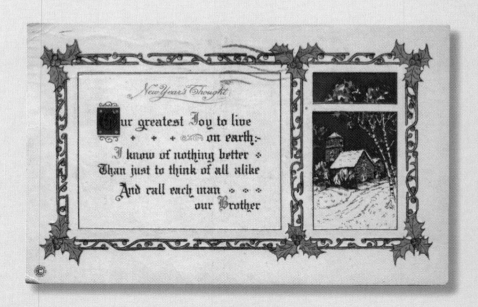

Church scene, $2.00 – 3.00.

Lamplighter, $3.00 – 4.00.

Glass, flowers, posted 1919, $3.00 – 4.00.

Best Wishes, $2.00 – 3.00.

Clock, bells, 1919, $3.00 – 4.00.

Holly, horseshoes, $2.00 – 3.00.

Couple greet, $4.00 – 5.00.

Mother, child, $2.00 – 3.00.

Horseshoe, bird, 1918, $3.00 – 4.00.

Couple hold hands, $4.00 – 5.00.

Christmas tree, $3.00 – 4.00.

Window, candle, $3.00 – 5.00.

Happy New Year, $2.00 – 3.00.

Boy, flowers, posted 1920, $12.00 – 15.00.

Bells, pine cones, $2.00 – 3.00.

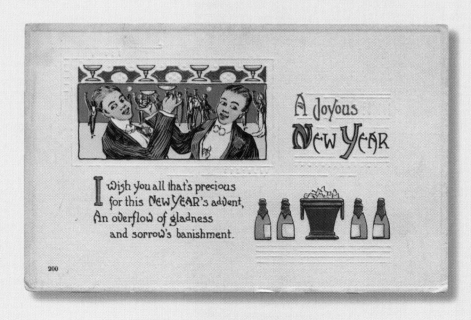

Men celebrate, $4.00 – 6.00.

A HAPPY NEW YEAR

May the New
Year hold for you
Good things old
and joys
new

Flowers, holly, $2.00 – 3.00.

A HAPPY NEW YEAR

Child in clock, $6.00 – 8.00.

WISHING YOU A TRULY
HAPPY NEW YEAR.

*Sorry I'm not with you to-day,
To utter my New Year's Greetings;
But hope ere twelve months pass away,
You and I will be meeting.* ∘∘

Truly Happy, posted 1921, $2.00 – 3.00.

Horseshoe, yellow roses,
$3.00 – 4.00.

My Very Best, $2.00 – 3.00.

Clock, candle, posted 1922,
$3.00 – 4.00.

Friendly New Year, $2.00 – 3.00.

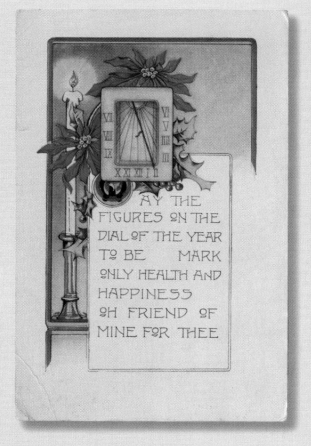

Flowers, clock, candle, posted 1922, $3.00 – 5.00.

Snow scene, $2.00 – 3.00.

Thank You, $3.00 – 4.00.

I Thank You and Wish
You a Happy New Year

I thank you for your wishes
For Christmas-tide, and pray
That you will find the New Year
Like one long happy day.

Grandfather clock, $3.00 – 4.00.

HAPPY NEW YEAR

Through the New Year
now appearing
May you have so much
that's cheering
That you smile a smile
a minute
From the time that you
begin it

Spring scene, $3.00 – 4.00.

WISHING YOU A HAPPY NEW YEAR

I'D HAVE YOU START THE
NEW YEAR RIGHT
YOU SEE AND SO I SEND
A WISH FOR SUNNY DAYS AND BRIGHT
TILL THIS NEW YEAR SHALL END

Bluebirds, posted 1923, $3.00 – 5.00.

Church steeple, $3.00 – 5.00.

Candle in window, $2.00 – 3.00.

HAPPY
NEW YEAR

When New Year Day has come around
I hope 'twill find you safe and sound,
Recovered from your Christmas mirth
And glad as if you owned the earth.

Cuckoo clock, posted 1925,
$3.00 – 5.00.

KIND NEW YEARS
GREETINGS

This New Years Day
I send to you
Kind loving thoughts
And Greetings true

Child at window, posted
1926, $3.00 – 5.00.

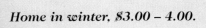

Home in winter, $3.00 – 4.00.

Wishing You a
Happy New Year

Bells, holly, posted 1927, $3.00 – 5.00.

Elegant birds, $3.00 – 4.00.

Ring Out Old, $2.00 – 3.00.

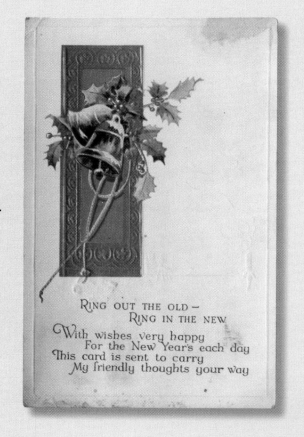

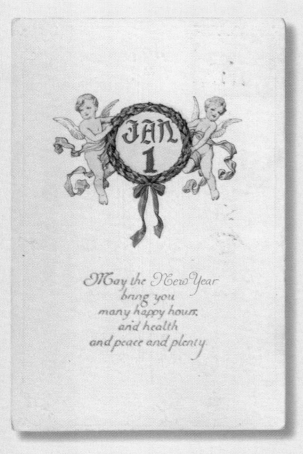

Winged figures, posted 1931, $4.00 – 5.00.

Pine trees, posted 1950, $2.00 – 3.00.

Flowers, posted 1949, $2.00 – 3.00.

Valentine's Day

This Heart of Violets sweet and meek,
Recall to me that I should seek
A Maiden's heart that's just as fine
And call it my dear Valentine.
Valentine postcard, 1910.

It follows that the tradition of giving valentines to those dear to us and the fascination with lovely postcards during the early twentieth century would make a fine romance.

As special events went in the early twentieth century, Valentine's Day was not even an official holiday although America already had established a long list of holidays. Still it was an occasion with a long tradition.

Certainly William Shakespear's Hamlet delighted audiences with references to St. Valentine's day and the valentine "maid at your window." As early as the six-

Comic scene, posted 1906, $3.00 – 5.00.

teenth century the event was in high favor and learned people wrote verses to their would-be valentines. Sometimes citizens in England and other European countries would draw names to determine who would be the participants' sweethearts for the remainder of the year.

Most sources credit valentine cards as being the first holiday greetings to be given wide distribution. It was, say some historians, the popularity of valentines in England which eventually gave rise to the production of decorated paper denoting various other holidays including Christmas. Some early Christmas greeting cards were in fact just valentine cards which had been further decorated (and edited) to include yuletide greetings instead of valentine romance. While this was certainly not the case of holiday postcards which came considerably later, many of the phrases were remarkably similar as was some of the festive artwork.

During the seventeenth century both men and women devoted hours of handiwork to preparing Valentine's Day messages of love. Images were often hand drawn or painted in water colors, carefully cut out, and then pasted together with bits of thread, lace, and silk.

Research shows the practice of actually dispatching attractive artwork valentines was fairly popular in England by the early 1700s and not surprisingly had become established in the American colonies by the 1740s. An example of this activity was displayed centuries later at a leading East Coast museum. The valentine on display was composed of a series of hand-drawn puzzle images attached to a single sheet of paper about six inches square. This interesting valentine, made around 1788, was signed T. Bailey. By the 1790s pictorial writing paper was available to further embellish homemade valentines and frequently symbols of flowers, birds, or hearts were added as further decoration and further sign of emotion. If need be, a tender message or verse could also be added.

At the dawn of the nineteenth century the movement in America and elsewhere was for ever more elaborate valentine messages with even finer examples of decoration. Scissors and fine pin pricks were used to imitate delicate lace, and sometimes an eager admirer added crewelwork and embroidery as well to the message. By 1803 the Dobbs Company of England was providing relatively fancy paper on a commercial basis for such uses. Eventually the company evolved into the rather extensive manufacture of valentines under such names as H. Dobbs and Company; Dobbs, Bailey, and Company; and later Dobbs, Kidd and Company.

It is worth noting that the Dobbs company valentines put heavy emphasis on flowers and Cupids along with their pressed silk and satin backings. By the late 1830s the firms in London were able to simulate lace from paper using hand-operated presses and thus the "new" layered look became available to the general public. Most of these things — flowers, Cupids, and layered lace would be seen again less than a century later on valentine postcards.

Back in the United States as the nineteenth century evolved the widespread use

Heart-shaped bouquet, posted 1907, $2.00 – 3.00.

of commercial valentines, for all of their striking appearance, would take still another decade to fully reach popularity. When the machine age arrived in America in the 1840s, there were a number of commercial firms producing exceptional valentines. Mailing valentines was still a very expensive proposition however, and in some cases the new-fangled envelopes could be almost as elaborate as the valentines themselves. American firms which were at last in the valentine business at this point included Turner & Fisher of Philadelphia, plus Charles Mangus, Elton and Company, and T.W. Strong, all of New York City. In later years they would be joined by P.J. Cozzens, the McLoughlin Brothers, J. Wrigley, and others.

In 1848, Strong, published the following newspaper advertisement:

Valentines! Valentines! All varieties of Valentines, imported and domestic, humorous, witty, comic...in the most superb manner, without regard to expense. Also envelopes and Valentine Writers, and everything connected with Valentines, to suit all customers. Prices vary from six cents to ten dollars; for sale wholesale and retail at Thomas W. Strong's.

Cupid, woman, posted 1907, $5.00 – 6.00.

During the 1850s Esther Howland of Worcester, Massachusetts became firmly established as a commercial fancy valentine producer in New England. The woman employed family, friends, and others to craft delightful valentines of paper lace with gilded backs and other creative touches. In later years the Howland cards were stamped on the back with either a red letter H or a white heart with a letter H centered on it. By the 1870s Howland had formed the prosperous New England Valentine Company which would eventually be owned and operated by George C. Whitney, a company employee.

Victorian valentines, both at home and abroad, became steadily more elaborate, whether store bought or home assembled with commercially purchased materials. By the 1890s mechanical cards and three-dimensional valentines were available in the United States, although the majority of the more advanced examples were being produced in Europe. And yet the greatest surge for valentines during the early 1900s came neither as a result of mechanical nor three-dimensional cards, instead it was single dimension valentine postcards.

Cupid atop world, $3.00 – 4.00.

Here at last were dazzling images being printed by the millions on handy mail-friendly postcards thanks in part to the advancing practice of chromolithography in Germany. Certainly the postcards gave a major boost to the already stylish idea of providing valentine greetings to others. The general availability of brightly colored valentine postcards in the marketplace meant dear hearts could now dispatch their feelings of sentiment much easier and far less expensively than ever before. Such postcards, with all their color and powers of illustration, also just added to the growing public feeling that valentines were indeed not just for lovers. They could now be dispatched to mothers, other family members, children, friends, and even neighbors. This expanding nature of valentines led to the frequent depiction of both children and Cupid on postcards. Moreover they featured an abundance of attractive young ladies, bouquets of flowers, and charming couples in costume. The couples were often very striking. Whether children or adults, the couples depicted were frequently shown dressed in their best

Cupid with heart, $4.00 – 5.00.

Heart of violets, $4.00 – 5.00.

clothing, or sometimes dressed in outfits of the Old West, American Indian, or some other era.

While valentine postcards prevailed on the landscape of early twentieth century America, they were not alone. Standard valentines were still being produced and consumed in an assortment of styles thanks to the efforts of such commercial leaders as Louis Prang, Elton and Company, and George Whitney which issued their own fancy layered cards right through the great postcard golden age. But for the most part the majority of Americans who expressed themselves during the first two decades of that century chose postcard valentines. A great number of the fine holiday postcard choices were still being printed in Germany, although the work of Raphael Tuck and Sons in England also had a significant impact on the trade.

The great love affair between the American public and the grand valentine postcard gradually faded in the 1920s. Such elegant postcards were still being manufactured and still in use, but they were certainly not seen in as great of numbers as before. Many people, once lured by the open postcard, were now following a post-World War I trend of using envelopes for their fancy valentines and other important messages.

Two Cupids, posted 1908, $8.00 – 10.00.

Cupid, flowers, posted 1908, $6.00 – 8.00.

Flowers, posted 1909, $2.00 – 3.00.

Cupid, lady, posted 1909, $6.00 – 8.00.

Valentine greeting, posted 1909, $2.00 – 3.00.

Three Cupids, corner clipped, $3.00 – 4.00.

Cupids, Raphael Tuck, $6.00 – 8.00.

I send to you this purple Bow
A loyal one I ween,
To pledge to you my vow
My Love, my Heart, my Queen.

Crowned Cupid, $3.00 – 5.00.

To my sweet little Valentine:

Let Cupid whisper in your ear
That you are my lady dear;
Then send him back on wings right swift,
To bring your heart — oh, welcome gift!

Couple in auto, $8.00 – 10.00.

To My Valentine

With Best Love

Child, flowers, $4.00 – 5.00.

Dove in heart, $3.00 – 4.00.

Cupid, quiver, $4.00 – 5.00.

Gift of Love, $3.00 – 4.00.

Cupid and bow, posted 1909,
$5.00 – 6.00.

Cupid, instrument, $5.00 – 6.00.

Cupid watering, 1909, $6.00 – 8.00.

Winged Cupid, $10.00 – 12.00.

Lady, Cupid, $5.00 – 6.00.

Costumed woman, $5.00 – 6.00.

Cupids with basket, $10.00 – 12.00.

Victorian lady, $8.00 – 10.00.

Cowboy Cupid, $8.00 – 10.00.

Woman, posted 1910, $4.00 – 5.00.

Be My Valentine, $2.00 – 3.00.

Cupid at window, $5.00 – 6.00.

Couple on boat, $3.00 – 5.00.

Clown, posted 1910, $6.00 – 8.00.

Love's Greeting, posted 1910, $5.00 – 6.00.

Cupid messenger, posted 1911,
$8.00 – 10.00.

Colonial children, $8.00 – 10.00.

Messenger with love,
$8.00 – 10.00.

Cupids, tree, $14.00 – 16.00.

Cupid with arrow, $5.00 – 6.00.

Colonial lady, posted 1911, $5.00 – 6.00.

Children, Cupid, $4.00 – 5.00.

Young woman, posted 1911, $5.00 – 6.00.

He'll Get You, $4.00 – 5.00.

Roses, 1911, $3.00 – 4.00.

Wishbone, hearts, $3.00 – 4.00.

Cupid, cherries, posted 1911, $4.00 – 5.00.

Sailing boats, $2.00 – 3.00.

**Love's Greetings, posted 1911,
$3.00 – 5.00.**

My True Valentine, $3.00 – 4.00.

Doves, Cupids, $6.00 – 8.00.

Flowers, $2.00 – 3.00.

Singing couple, posted 1911, $5.00 – 6.00.

Cupid's Message, posted 1911, $4.00 – 5.00.

Little Valentine, $3.00 – 4.00.

Cupid, balcony, posted 1911, $8.00 – 10.00.

Couple, garden wall, $6.00 – 8.00.

Youngster, Raphael Tuck, $5.00 – 6.00.

Cupid in chains, $3.00 – 5.00.

Heart, flowers, $2.00 – 3.00.

Heart bouquet, $3.00 – 4.00.

Couple, seaside, 1911, $6.00 – 8.00.

Now lest you should be watching, When I come to your door With this expression of true love These hearts, one-two-three-four, I'll just conceal my smiling face For it is not quite right To let one's SWEETHEART know that she Loves him with all her might.

MHS.

25

Girl, umbrella, $4.00 – 5.00.

To my true Valentine.

Girl in bonnet, posted 1912, $5.00 – 6.00.

To my Valentine

To My Valentine, $3.00 – 4.00.

Airplane, Cupid, 1912, $16.00 – 18.00.

Cupid and anvil, posted 1912, $8.00 – 10.00.

Cupid, double hearts, $6.00 – 8.00.

Costumed couple, posted 1912, $8.00 – 10.00.

Valentine Message, $2.00 – 3.00.

Love's Offering, $3.00 – 4.00.

Valentine Serenade,
$6.00 – 8.00.

I send love to sing a sweet **Valentine Serenade** before the window of your heart to which I hope will listen for my sake.

Large heart, posted 1912,
$6.00 – 8.00.

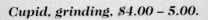

Cupid, grinding, $4.00 – 5.00.

Lady, Cupid, posted 1912, $5.00 – 6.00.

A Game, couple, $18.00 – 20.00.

Paeonia symbol, $2.00 – 3.00.

**If Storms, posted 1913,
$4.00 – 5.00.**

Dear Heart, $3.00 – 4.00.

Arrow, heart, $3.00 – 4.00.

Sincerely, I Greet, $6.00 – 8.00.

Room For Two, $12.00 – 16.00.

Flower arrangement, $3.00 – 4.00.

Cupid, $4.00 – 5.00.

Dove, heart, $3.00 – 5.00.

Dutch couple, $5.00 – 6.00.

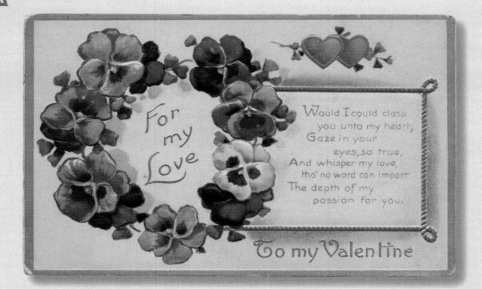

For My Love, $2.00 – 3.00.

Dove, letter, posted 1914, $6.00 – 8.00.

Cupid, children, posted 1914, $6.00 – 8.00.

Dutch children, $8.00 – 10.00.

Young woman, posted 1917, $6.00 – 8.00.

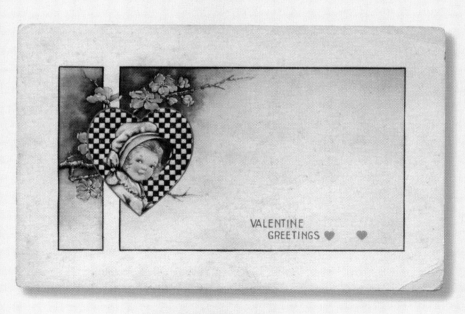

Girl in bonnet, $2.00 – 3.00.

Costumed girl, $4.00 – 5.00.

To My Valentine, $4.00 – 5.00.

My Heart, $2.00 – 3.00.

Woman at wheel, $3.00 – 5.00.

Friendship, $3.00 – 4.00.

Couple, candy, $5.00 – 6.00.

My Heart Is Big, $5.00 – 6.00.

Girl, kitten, posted 1920s, $4.00 – 5.00.

Girls skating, posted 1924, $3.00 – 4.00.

Valentine Greeting,
$2.00 – 3.00.

PLEASE BE MY
VALENTINE

O don't you think
It would be fine
To try this on
Your Valentine?

Couple kissing, $3.00 – 5.00.

On Valentine's Day
The trail of lonesome hearts,
my dear,
Is very long indeed,
So let me safely guide you
Where Cupid's footsteps
lead!

Indian couple, posted 1923,
$4.00 – 6.00.

Couple, heart, posted 1926,
$3.00 – 5.00.

Rooster, chicks, posted 1928,
$3.00 – 6.00.

Young woman, posted 1941,
$3.00 – 5.00.

Presidents' Day

Greetings from Los Angeles, posted 1906, $6.00 – 8.00.

In the early morning of February 19, 1906, an enthusiastic supporter sent a George Washington birthday greetings postcard from California. The card, with an oval image of Washington and hand-painted cherry tree branches, was carefully scripted with Greetings from Los Angeles.

It was but one of many George Washington birthday greetings postcards prepared privately and commercially in the heyday of such mailings. Typically the American eagle, American flag, the cherry tree, or Washington's home, Mount Vernon, were featured on them. Most were quite graphic and highly patriotic during the early 1900s. Later some versions included Washington and his wife Martha at Mount Vernon or some aspect of the Washington Monument in Washington, D.C.

Washington, America's first national hero and first president, was, of course, born in February of 1732 in Westmoreland County, Virginia. While he lost his father when he was only nine years of age, Washington went on to become a military leader and eventually president of the United States.

Unlike most of the rest of America's presidents, Washington's birthday was a national event even while the noted leader was alive. One New York newspaper account published in the 1780s observed, "Wednesday last being the birthday of his Excellency, George Washington, the same was celebrated here by all the true friends of American Independence and constitutional Liberty, with that hilarity and manly decorum ever attendant on the sons of freedom."

It added further, "in the evening an entertainment was given on board the East India ship in this harbor to a very brilliant and respectable company, and a discharge of thirteen cannon was fired on this joyful occasion."

Historical accounts suggest that Washington's birthday was first given governmental endorsement in 1792 when Congress approved a motion to adjourn one half hour in his honor. Bear in mind that Washington was not only alive but

Washington's Birthday Greetings, $10.00 – 14.00.

From Mt. Vernon, $7.00 – 8.00.

quite healthy as well. The first president died during the last month of the last year of the eighteenth century after a relatively brief illness. By the early 1800s a number of memorial items, including handkerchiefs, had been issued in remembrance of the great leader.

The emerging use of postcards early in the twentieth century some 100 years later meant still more attractive tributes to the person who was known as the father of our country. Leading postcard artists contributed their renderings, and some others simply reproduced an image of Washington.

Abraham Lincoln was also born in the month of February in 1809 just ten years after the death of George Washington. Lincoln was born in Hardin County, Kentucky. Lincoln lost his mother when he was only seven years old. He went on to become a rail-splitter and legislator before being elected president of the United States. After four years of bitter civil war, Lincoln was the victim of assassination in April 1865.

Immediately after his death Lincoln was immortalized with all manner of memorabilia, and by the early 1900s, the deceased president was depicted on postcards. Like the postcards representing Washington, the postcards of Lincoln drew offerings from leading artists as well as from those lesser known. Many were very striking and patriotic like those which had paid tribute to Washington. Others simply featured Lincoln's life from its beginning in a simple log cabin to the White House. In later years other Lincoln postcards illustrated his Gettysburg address and scenes from the Lincoln National Historic Park in Hodgenville, Kentucky.

Interestingly enough while both Washington and Lincoln were celebrated on postcards during the earliest decades of the twentieth century, they were not accepted equally. In 1919 most all existing states observed Washington's birthday as a holiday along with Puerto Rico and Alaska (which of course was not a state at the time). An exception was Mississippi according to one leading encyclopedia of the period, but "it is observed, however, in the public schools of the latter state."

By contrast Lincoln's birthday held holiday status

Miniature portraits, Martha and George, $6.00 – 8.00.

only in northern and western states in 1919. Even ten years later in 1929 only West Virginia had been added to the rather selective list of states officially observing the holiday.

As events and governmental action would have it the two events would both be merged into a single holiday known formally as Presidents' Day. It was not exactly the way it was planned. In 1968 an act of congress officially degreed that Washington's birthday would be observed on the third Monday of February instead of any specific date. The idea was to give the public a three-day weekend instead of just an idle day in the middle of a winter month. The Congress, at the same time, also acted to make three more federal holidays parts of three day weekend packages as well. Also given such status at the time were Memorial Day, Veterans' Day, and Columbus Day.

So students of history may still be wondering how then did Washington's birthday observance

Lincoln crowning, $10.00 – 12.00.

also manage to include Lincoln and the rest of the presidents? In February of 1971 Richard Nixon signed a presidential proclamation declaring the Washington holiday to be Presidents' Day, "the first such three-day holiday set aside to honor all presidents, even myself."

Years later the famed *USA Today* national newspaper took issue with the whole thing and observed, "apparently unaware that presidential proclamations do not supersede the rule of law, the nation pushed Washington to the background and came to observe the day as Nixon decreed."

In the year 2000 President Bill Clinton also got into the act with his own proclamation declaring the event as a day when "we salute the leadership and achievements of all those who have held America's highest elective office." Since then there have been efforts in Congress to return the day to one which simply celebrated the birthday of George Washington.

Log cabin, White House, $15.00 – 18.00.

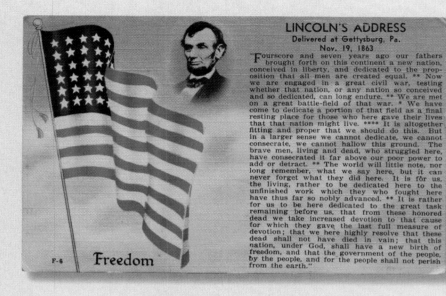

Lincoln's Address, $5.00 – 7.00.

Lincoln birthplace, $3.00 – 5.00.

St. Patrick's Day

"St. Patrick was a Gentleman."

Irish youngster, Clapsaddle, damaged, $4.00 – 5.00.

Saint Patrick's Day is considered a time for the wearing of the green and for the celebration of any real or imagined Irish heritage. While the legend of St. Patrick has abounded for centuries, the Americanized observance of the holiday did not really flourish until the onset of the twentieth century.

Originally the date of March 17 was set aside to pay tribute to the patron saint of Ireland, but gradually the event evolved into what has become more of an observance of the full Irish tradition.

In Ireland, St. Patrick's Day is a church holiday, and it honors the man credited with bringing Christianity into the Emerald Isle. Historic accounts say St. Patrick was not actually born in Ireland but instead was captured by pirates and sold into Irish slavery sometime prior to 400 A.D. As a youngster St. Patrick was said to have herded swine and helped with farming. As an adult Patrick was credited with doing great deeds for the people of Ireland as well as rising in the ranks of the Catholic church under the name Patricius.

Besides all the good deeds, St. Patrick also was given great agricultural significance as well in Ireland. Frequently stock was driven out into the summer pastures on the holiday. An old Irish saying notes, "Saint Patrick turns the warm side of the stone uppermost," and farmers are prone to start planting their potatoes on that specific holiday.

Among the most famous deeds linked to the legend of St. Patrick is the driving out of all the snakes in Ireland. A popular Irish song at the turn of the twentieth century contained this line:

He drove the frogs into bogs and banished all the vermin.

At any rate the Irish saint had a significant following in America early on. Reportedly the first charitable Irish organization in colonial America was formed in Boston on March 17, 1737, as tribute to St. Patrick. On yet another St. Partick's Day, American troops were able to recapture the city of Boston from the British during the Revolutionary War. General George Washington was said to have selected the word Boston as the password for the operation, with St. Patrick being the responding countersign.

New York City began hosting mammoth St. Patrick Day parades by the latter eighteenth century but widespread observance of the event was not evident in the United States until more than a century later when extending Irish-related greetings to others was popular.

By the early 1900s postcards were mirroring the public's fondness for St. Patrick's Day. The postcards often featured the very things of the St. Patrick stories and legend including green top hats, children, St. Patrick as a youngster, the Paddy pig or just pigs, dancing of an Irish jig, pots of gold and the leprechauns that supposedly knew where such pots were hidden, clay pipes, harps, scenes of the Irish countryside, and of course the shamrock.

The shamrock was by far the most favored of the Irish symbols for celebrations early in the twentieth century. In 1917 author J. Walker McSpadden observed in *The Book of Holidays*, "thousands of those little fabric shamrocks are sold along the streets of America on Saint Patick's Day in

Irish clay pipe, Clapsaddle, $6.00 – 8.00.

the morning." Thousands of shamrocks appeared as illustrations on postcards of that era too.

Other postcards for that event featured the flag of Ireland, or perhaps a combination of the American and Irish flags. The white harp which figured on many of the St. Patrick's Day postcards represented the white harp depicted on the national flag of Ireland. Frequently the postcards also carried non-English but none-the-less ageless slogans such as *Beannact Dia leat* (God Bless you), and the famed *Erin go braugh* (Ireland forever).

A number of the leading artists of the day contributed their efforts to St. Patrick's Day postcards including Ellen Clapsaddle and Frances Brundage. Other artists included H.B. Griggs, Mary Evans Price, and Samuel L. Smucker. Clapsaddle was probably the most prolific with her Irish children, charming young women in bonnets, and even Irish infants.

Like so many other holiday greeting postcards, a great number were printed in Germany, followed by the United States, Italy, and finally England. Some postcard publishers were located in more than one place, the distinguished Raphael Tuck and Sons, for example, had offices in London, Berlin, and New York. Alas, few if any St. Patrick's Day postcards were ever actually printed in Ireland. Moreover few of the "Irish" postcards were even distributed in Ireland despite their adoration in the United States.

Young Irish man, $6.00 – 8.00.

Best Wishes, $2.00 – 3.00.

Shamrock,   pipe,
$4.00 – 5.00.

Pipes, scene, posted 1910,
$5.00 – 6.00.

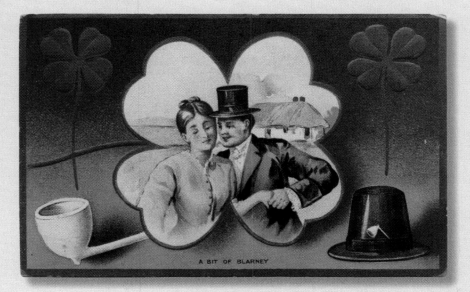

Irish couple, $5.00 – 7.00.

Irish jig, $4.00 – 6.00.

Various symbols, posted 1910, $4.00 – 5.00.

Irish woman, dated 1910, $5.00 – 6.00.

Irish man, dated 1910, $5.00 – 6.00.

Irish humor, $5.00 – 6.00.

Tho' the last glimpse of Erin with sorrow I see
Yet wherever thou art shall seem Erin to me:
In exile thy bosom shall still be my home,
And thine eyes make my climate wherever
we roam.   MOORE.

ST. PATRICK'S DAY
GREETINGS

Greetings, $5.00 – 6.00.

Killarney

"She's not a dull or cold land;
No! she's a warm and
bold land;
Oh! she's a true and
old land—
This native land of mine."

Killarney, Clapsaddle, damaged,
$2.00 – 3.00.

St. Patrick's Day
Greetings

Pipe, dated 1911, $5.00 – 6.00.

Dear Irish, $3.00 – 4.00.

Golden harp, $3.00 – 4.00.

Cappaquin Co., posted 1911, $5.00 – 6.00.

Handshake, damaged, $2.00 – 3.00.

Four-leaf clover, posted 1914, $5.00 – 6.00.

Saintly theme, posted 1911, $5.00 – 6.00.

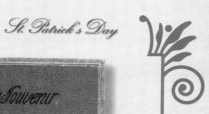

Souvenir, $5.00 – 6.00.

Mangerten   Mountain
$5.00 – 6.00.

Lake Killarney, $5.00 – 6.00.

Easter

Easter has been observed worldwide for hundreds of years, but it was not seen as a significant commercial event in America until the second half of the nineteenth century. Ultimately that commercial coming-of-age in America led to the robust publication of colorful Easter postcards.

Easter is observed in relationship to the first full moon following the vernal equinox of the year. This makes the special Sunday vary year to year from late March to the middle of April. Scholars generally

Eastertide angel, posted 1905, $4.00 – 5.00.

agree that early Christians had managed to work their own religious observance into the time of the ongoing Roman festival for the goddess Eastre. By doing so the Christians avoided drawing attention to themselves which likely would have led to further religious persecution.

There are many variations of Easter's original name including the goddess name Eastre, and variations such as Eostur and Eastur. Some accounts credit Norsemen with a similar Easter-like word meaning the season of the growing sun. At any rate it was a word familiar in Anglo-Saxon usage for more than 20 centuries.

As early as 669 the Archbishop of England made the first full moon rule previously mentioned an official practice. This particular full moon was eventually known as the Paschal moon, because it took place at the time of the Jewish Passover. Some centuries later in 1752 the English Church in Great Britain adopted their own calendar, which brought them into alignment with the earlier religious edict. However others including the churches of Russia and Greece did not reflect the change and observed Easter on still another Sunday.

The arrival of the Easter rabbit into the observation is somewhat more controversial. One theory suggests that the rabbit or hare was the earthly form for the goddess Eastre. Thus when such an animal was sighted during the spring season it was sure to be goddess Eastre herself. Still another theory links the rabbit as a powerful symbol of fertility with ancient Egypt.

Chicks dressed, posted 1906, $8.00 – 9.00.

It was believed that Egyptians used the image of the rabbit on their royal tombs because of the animal's supposed powers of fertility. One legend in the Far East held that a female rabbit was so fertile that she could become pregnant simply by staring at the full moon. Meanwhile others point to the fact that the ancient Chinese believed that rabbits lived very long lives. When rabbits reached the age of 100 they turned white, and by the time they reached 500 yeas of age their fur turned blue.

Whatever the origin, the basic Easter bunny hopped up again in Germany by the early 1700s where it was said to have delivered gifts to children. Some said it was a means for wealthy or well-placed people to somehow reward neighboring children with gifts or simply chicken's eggs. To make them more appealing and attractive the eggs were brightly colored and placed in wooded areas for children to find. As the children sought out the eggs they were likely to see a rabbit skittering

Chicks, umbrella, posted 1907, $5.00 – 6.00.

across their path, and thus the long-eared animal was linked fondly to the treasured eggs left behind. This theme was certainly brought to practice in America when Pennsylvania-German settlers celebrated Oschter Haws with children from the dawn of the eighteenth century.

In 1928 an updated version was offered by Clara Denton in the refreshing book, *New Year's to Christmas in Holiday Land:*

"You will often see pictures of rabbits on Easter postcards and you will naturally wonder why they are there, but it comes from a very old myth.

"The hare is the ancient symbol, or figure, of the moon, and as Easter day is governed by the moon, the hare must enter into all Easter representations. Hares, unlike rabbits, are born with their eyes open, and the moon is the open-eyed watcher of the night. And as there are no hares in this country (United States), we accept the rabbit as a substitute."

Certainly the practice of giving colorful Easter eggs, which had been long established in Germany and other European countries, was very popular early in twentieth century America just as darling

Loving Easter, posted 1907, Tuck & Sons, $4.00 – 6.00.

postcards made their appearance on the cultural scene. Printed initially in Germany and later in the United States, Easter postcards lent themselves to lithographic printing. Such images in the form of Easter greetings could now be sent by mail to someone else far away.

Certainly the Easter rabbit was a major figure on holiday postcards. Sometimes the rabbits were depicted wearing the clothing of humans, and even more frequently they were paired with chickens in some sort of gala scene with a brief message.

The use of color in Easter greeting postcards made them all the more striking. One, posted 1910, featured chicks in a wheelbarrow along with a decorated Easter egg. It bore this verse:

> *The oddest chick I've ever seen,*
> *Had feathers pink and blue and green;*
> *A crimson beak, a purple leg,*
> *'Twas hatched out from an Easter egg.*

Elsewhere chicks disembarked from an air balloon, or a chick dressed as a clown, or chicks and a rabbit nested together in a man's dapper straw hat. Children were frequently depicted on the postcards as well, sometimes with chicks and sometimes with rabbits. Children might be shown holding decorated Easter eggs or happily riding in a "modern" automobile.

Ironically, even though the holiday had deeply religious origins, relatively few religious holiday postcards were published for Easter. Some featured Jesus Christ or gave heavy emphasis to the Christian symbol of the cross, but more were likely to hold to non-secular themes such as groupings of lovely flowers or scenes from the countryside. An occasional angel might be found on an Easter postcard, and sometimes a little boy in top hat looking more like the New Year's Baby than an Easter child would appear.

Easter flowers, posted 1907, $2.00 – 4.00.

Chicks in egg, posted 1907, $3.00 – 5.00.

Riley roses, posted 1907,
$2.00 – 3.00.

Lambs, cart, child,
$8.00 – 11.00.

Chick as jester, posted 1907,
$7.00 – 8.00.

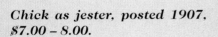

Children in costume, $7.00 – 8.00.

Chick on egg, $3.00 – 4.00.

Cross, star, flowers, Tuck & Sons, $3.00 – 4.00.

Hen, chicks, posted 1908,
$3.00 – 4.00.

Dutch boy, chicks, $5.00 – 7.00.

Hen, chicks, noisemaker,
$10.00 – 12.00.

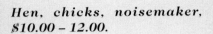

Cross, flowers, posted 1909, $3.00 – 4.00.

Rooster, hen, $4.00 – 5.00.

Chick, egg, posted 1909, $4.00 – 5.00.

Four chicks, Tuck & Sons, $4.00 – 5.00.

Flowers, cottage, $2.00 – 3.00.

Chickens, colored eggs, $6.00 – 8.00.

Vase, flowers, Tuck & Sons, $3.00 – 4.00.

Rabbit, chick, posted 1909, $10.00 – 12.00.

Rabbits, staw hat, $8.00 – 11.00.

Chicks, airship, $22.00 – 26.00.

Cross, flowers, posted 1909, $3.00 – 4.00.

Chick, wheelbarrow, $18.00 – 20.00.

Flowers, bag, $3.00 – 4.00.

Rabbit, egg, chick,
$8.00 – 9.00.

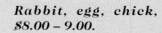

Chicks with hats, corner
damaged, $5.00 – 6.00.

Chicks, egg, $6.00 – 8.00.

The oddest chick I've ever seen,
Had feathers pink and blue and green;
A crimson beak, a purple leg,
'Twas hatched out from an Easter-egg.

Colored chick with verse,
$6.00 – 8.00.

Little girl, chicks, creased,
$4.00 – 5.00.

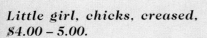

Easter child, $5.00 – 6.00.

Child, rabbit, artist signed, $12.00 – 15.00.

Chicks, gift box, $6.00 – 7.00.

Chicks, egg, $4.00 – 5.00.

Rabbit, cart of eggs, $8.00 – 10.00.

Cracked egg view, posted 1909, $6.00 – 8.00.

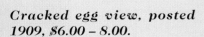

Child and lamb, $5.00 – 6.00.

Angels and cross, $6.00 – 8.00.

Child and lambs, $6.00 – 8.00.

Decorated egg, $3.00 – 4.00.

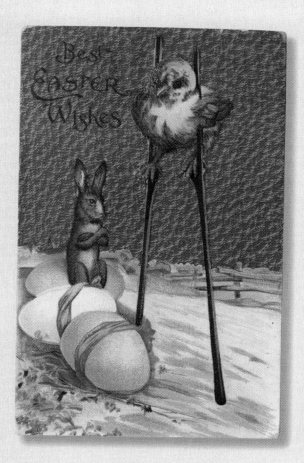

Chick on stilts, posted 1911, $8.00 – 10.00.

Eggs, flowers, Tuck & Sons, $3.00 – 4.00.

Chicks, egg, posted 1910, $3.00 – 4.00.

Rooster, rabbit, $6.00 – 8.00.

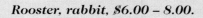

Child, Easter egg basket, $10.00 – 12.00.

Chick and egg, $3.00 – 4.00.

Here's an Easter bunnie.
I'm bringing him to you.
I hope he will not just decide
To scramble out.
Don't
you?

Child, rabbit in basket, $8.00 – 10.00.

Best Wishes for Easter.

Chick, cottage, posted 1910, $3.00 – 4.00.

Christ and banner, $5.00 – 6.00.

Chickens and chicks, $5.00 – 6.00.

Cross and rose, $3.00 – 4.00.

Choir boy sings, $4.00 – 5.00.

Lambs and cross, $4.00 – 6.00.

Duckling and bird, $4.00 – 6.00.

Rooster, hens, chicks, $5.00 – 6.00.

Flowers and chicks, $3.00 – 4.00.

Pair of rabbits, $4.00 – 5.00.

Cross and flowers, $3.00 – 4.00.

Silvered cross, flowers, $3.00 – 4.00.

Flowers in basket, $3.00 – 4.00.

Rabbits and chicks,
$4.00 – 5.00.

Chicks about pail,
$5.00 – 6.00.

Chicks in slippers,
$4.00 – 5.00.

Chick on straw hat, $6.00 – 8.00.

Choirboy in flower, $2.00 – 3.00.

Flowers with cross, $2.00 – 3.00.

Woman and bouquet, $3.00 – 4.00.

Chicks in basket, posted 1911, $4.00 – 5.00.

Rooster and hen, $3.00 – 4.00.

Chicks in decorated dish, $5.00 – 6.00.

Cross, shepherd, $2.00 – 3.00.

Brown and white rabbit,
$4.00 – 5.00.

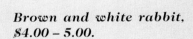

**Chickens and eggs,
$3.00 – 4.00.**

**Rabbit and basket, posted
1912, $3.00 – 4.00.**

**Child, cart, rabbits,
$10.00 – 12.00.**

Flowers and cottage, $2.00 – 3.00.

Chick holds flower, $3.00 – 4.00.

Rabbits on seesaw, posted 1912, $8.00 – 10.00.

Sings Easter hymn, $5.00 – 6.00.

Chicks in egg, posted 1912, $4.00 – 5.00.

Rabbit in jacket, $6.00 – 8.00.

Spring flowers, posted 1913, $3.00 – 5.00.

Long-eared rabbit, $6.00 – 8.00.

Vase and rabbit, $3.00 – 4.00.

Flowers and cross, $2.00 – 3.00.

Easter Blessings, $4.00 – 5.00.

Rabbit, colored eggs, $6.00 – 8.00.

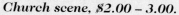

Church scene, $2.00 – 3.00.

Holy Easter day, $3.00 – 4.00.

Hen and chicks, $4.00 – 6.00.

Child and chickens, $5.00 – 6.00.

Rooster and colored eggs, $5.00 – 6.00.

Chickens and chicks, posted 1913, $5.00 – 6.00.

Child in costume, $6.00 – 8.00.

Chicks circle decorated tree, $6.00 – 8.00.

Easter angel, $5.00 – 7.00.

Angel and flowers, $5.00 – 6.00.

Easter service, $4.00 – 5.00.

Children, decorated eggs, $6.00 – 8.00.

Pair of Easter chicks,
$5.00 – 6.00.

Chicks in gift box,
$6.00 – 8.00.

Rabbit with song scroll,
$6.00 – 8.00.

Rabbit, flowers, $3.00 – 4.00.

Chick and cross, $4.00 – 5.00.

Flowers in rowboat, $2.00 – 3.00.

Woman holds lamb, posted 1914,
$6.00 – 8.00.

Chicks behind egg, $5.00 – 6.00.

Multicolored chick, posted 1914, $6.00 – 8.00.

White rabbit, posted 1915, $8.00 – 10.00.

Stylish woman, $4.00 – 5.00.

Chicks and mirror, damaged, $3.00 – 4.00.

Angel, singing chick,
$5.00 – 6.00.

Chick, multicolored egg,
$8.00 – 10.00.

Host of angels, $5.00 – 6.00.

Rabbit, basket of eggs, $6.00 – 8.00.

Youngster in top hat, $7.00 – 8.00.

Happy Easter, posted 1916, $2.00 – 4.00.

Children and eggs,
$7.00 – 8.00.

Butterflies, verse, $3.00 – 4.00.

Children in robes,
$4.00 – 5.00.

**Girls on automobile,
$8.00 – 10.00.**

**Chick wears eggshell,
$4.00 – 5.00.**

**Rabbit and chicks,
$6.00 – 8.00.**

Rabbit, pink bonnet box, posted 1922, $8.00 – 10.00.

Child, basket, rabbit, $8.00 – 10.00.

Chick and frog, posted 1923, $6.00 – 8.00.

Child feeds chickens,
$6.00 – 8.00.

Rabbits in hat box,
$7.00 – 8.00.

Rabbits pull eggs,
$8.00 – 10.00.

Girl, basket, rabbit,
$6.00 – 8.00.

Chick, Easter egg, posted
1924, $6.00 – 8.00.

Rabbit human clothing,
$30.00 – 35.00.

Gowned woman, flowers, posted 1918,
$5.00 – 6.00.

Easter Rose, posted 1930, $4.00 – 5.00.

Rabbit wearing jacket, posted 1930, $8.00 – 10.00.

Patriotic Holidays

German-American, posted 1905,
$6.00 – 8.00.

Displays of patriotism abounded in the United States long before the arrival of holiday postcards early in the twentieth century. Yet the robust stars and stripes and all those related images just never looked better than they did in print on illustrated postcards.

Within ten years of the "new" century citizens were busy buying and mailing patriotic postcards of all types. Sometimes the images were of children decked out in clothing of red, white, and blue. Others featured lovely women in fashionable dresses and soldiers in crisp military uniforms. Almost every one of the patriotic postcards included a brightly colored American flag to help set the stirring scene.

Looking back in 1973, a leading publication on antiques and collectibles noted that this special group of postcards were known as "patriotics" among collectors. They were to be distinguished in part by their attention to such holidays as Decoration/Memorial Day, Flag Day, and Independence Day. Such cards of the immediate past, said the *Antiques Journal,* "depicted American customs and ways of life. Children were shown dressed in Buster Brown costumes or sailor attire...winsome girls wore long tresses" and mothers wore flowing dresses with picturesque hats and "bowed slippers" in Gibson girl style. Moreover there was Miss Liberty, an attraction on many of the patriotic postcards, nearly always clad in white but often with a further touch of red and blue.

If the striking images were not heartfelt enough, there was usually a message as well such as "when can their glory fade," or "my country tis of thee."

As with other holiday postcards, a number of artists contributed their skills to the cause of patriotism. One of the most significant was Ellen Clapsaddle with sketches of children and adults all proclaiming the glory of Americanism. In time her postcard illustrations saluted everything from the veterans of the Grand Army of the Republic to the Fourth of July itself. Most adored were those of children holding or waving U.S. flags. Another strong contributor was C. Chapman whose Memorial Day illustrations were especially impressive.

Among the leading publishers of patriotic postcards one of the most significant was the legendary Raphael Tuck Company (later Tuck and Sons) which literally had a worldwide audience. Tuck tended to single out American heroes of the past including General U.S. Grant. Typical Tuck cards of patriotism had pictures ranging from happy children to white-bearded veterans of the Civil War. Tuck, and a few other publishers, liked the patriotic holidays well enough to issue a number of series of postcards featuring historic or contemporary aspects of the events as they were viewed in the early 1900s.

The Raphael Tuck Company (offices in New York, Berlin, and London) could not seem to solve the dilemma whether to regard May 30 as Decoration Day or Memorial Day. Actually Tuck and many other postcard publishers of the early twentieth century used both designations at virtually the same time. Some issues were simply marked Decoration Day while others heralded Memorial Day instead.

Most accounts indicate Decoration Day came first, linking it to a time during and immediately after the Civil War when southern women reportedly decorated the graves of both Confederate and Union soldiers. A few other accounts disagree on the origins of the event, but at any rate it was made official in 1868 when U.S. Army Commander General John A. Logan decreed such a day:

The day, for the purpose of strewing with flowers or otherwise decorating the graves of comrades who died in defense of their country, and whose bodies now lie in almost every city, village, or hamlet church yard in the land.... It is the purpose of the commander-in-chief to inaugurate this observance with the hope that it will be kept from year to year while a survivor of the war remains to honor the memory of the departed.

By the early 1900s the legal holiday was mostly designated as Memorial Day and it was observed by law in most northern states. A Confederate Memorial Day was also legally observed in a number of states, while a few instead observed the birthday of Confederate president Jefferson Davis.

Despite the legal references, the confusion over the holiday's official name continued. In 1917 author J. Walker McSpadden offered that the popular name of Decoration Day was "the better designation for this holiday. A memorial day could be kept without flow-

Women, children, $8.00 – 10.00.

ers; a decoration day cannot, and this is the day we offer flowers for our soldier dead." McSpadden may have had a good point, but latter generations put aside the Decoration Day title almost entirely for the slightly newer Memorial Day which likely indicates the American public's tendency to celebrate the event more with parades and speeches rather than visiting graveyards.

Flag Day had quite a different origin. As previously mentioned the American flag was a favorite subject of the United States postcard market from the beginning and that feeling, and its connected patriotism, escalated immediately prior to World War I.

The first official Flag Day was proclaimed in 1917 by President Woodrow Wilson who specified it would be observed on June 30 of each year. Legend at the time said that seamstress Betsy Ross had helped direct the design of the American flag when General George Washington visited her at 239 Arch Street in Philadelphia. Washington and others, as the story goes, felt a six-point star would be best on the flag while Ross held a five-point star would be less "English" and therefore more American. Early postcards not only often featured the flag, but sometimes also called attention to the "Birthplace of Old Glory" at the Betsy Ross house in Philadelphia.

By the time of World War II in the 1940s there was great fervor of American patriotism and correspondingly the renewed use of the flag on numerous postcards. Today collections of such cards tend to expand to include the entire half century of their reign.

Accordingly Independence Day was a big attraction for celebrations and for holiday postcards during the first quarter of the twentieth century.

Typically Independence Day or Fourth of July postcard themes dealt with firecrackers exploding or at least about to be set off and exploded. Sometimes they depicted colorful Uncle Sam, and sometimes they just featured children having fun on the glorious fourth. Certainly the postcard publishers of that era did not view children handling fireworks with the alarm that would be present today. Not only were fireworks quite legal a century ago, but they were quite abundant nationwide.

Miss Liberty, Chapman, $12.00 – 18.00.

In Memoriam, posted 1913, $5.00 – 6.00.

Decoration Day series, Tuck, $5.00 – 6.00.

Soldier, flag, $6.00 – 8.00.

Soldier, sweetheart, Selige, $5.00 – 6.00.

Two generations, $8.00 – 10.00.

Soldier, flag, posted 1918,
$4.00 – 5.00.

American flag, copyright
1909, $3.00 – 4.00.

Flag, Loyality series,
$2.00 – 3.00.

Betsy Ross house, $3.00 – 4.00.

Flag series, Tichnor, 1940, $3.00 – 5.00.

Our Flag, posted 1917, $3.00 – 5.00.

Flag, Curt Teich, posted 1942, $2.00 – 3.00.

Stars and Stripes, 4th, $25.00 – 28.00.

Flag & country, posted 1918, $5.00 – 6.00.

July Fourth, posted 1911, $8.00 – 10.00.

Happy Fourth, $35.00 – 45.00.

Halloween

Historically speaking Halloween may well be the oldest holiday to be observed in the United States, certainly it predates any other established event on the modern calendar.

Probably even more important is the fact that collectors treasure holiday greeting postcards of Halloween above all others. It is not that Halloween postcards are the grandest of all. Actually the same artists and publishers combined talents for other holiday postcards as well, but Halloween and everything related to it remains the most collectible of all American holidays.

In ancient times October 31 or thereabouts was the last day of the year on the Celtic calendar. A festival honoring Samhain, the Celtic lord of death, began that evening. When the Celts were conquered by the Romans, two of their autumn festivals were combined with Samhain.

During the latter part of the nineteenth century the celebration of Halloween was more of an event for adults than for children. The more affluent Victorian households

Black cat, witch, $30.00 – 35.00.

hosted black cat holiday parties where festivities for grown-ups included jumping over candles, fortune telling, and bobbing for apples. Not too surprisingly black cats and party activities had a major role in Halloween postcards which followed in the early 1900s. By the time greeting postcards became popular, Halloween was already firmly established in the American culture. If anything it may have tilted more toward children than grown-ups with the arrival of the new century, but it was still a big event.

It just seemed that the artistry of Halloween postcards was to merge with the affection the public had for the holiday. The printed cards were a delight of symbols and color, and mailing all that to friend or loved one only cost a penny. Artists like Ellen Clapsaddle, Frances Brundage, and E.C. Banks allied themselves with such publishers as Tuck, Art Publishing Company, and Wolf Brothers for stunning results. Halloween postcards flourished generally from early 1900 to 1930, although a few still remained in vogue clear up until the

Witch on broom, posted 1911,
$25.00 – 28.00.

1940s. Along with witches and black cats, a major item on Halloween postcards was the jack-o-lantern. In 1911 the *Volume Library* observed that such glowing pumpkin standards were part of an old custom, "still observed in some places, to drive away the spirits of darkness supposed to be hoving in the air."

Irish folklore specifically mentioned a fellow named Jack who ended up condemned to darkness and was accorded but a single lump of burning coal. Legend had it that Jack carved a turnip and carried the glowing ember about in the darkness. An Americanization of the yarn found parents providing the much more plentiful and seasonal pumpkin instead of the distant turnip to go along with the account in this country. The same *Volume Library* maintained however that it was not Ireland but rather England and Scotland that were better known for the "superstitious tradition" of Halloween. The reference book advised youngsters, "on this mystic evening it was believed that the human spirit was enabled, by the aid of supernatural power, to detach itself from the body and wander through the realms of space."

At any rate all of these things, along with a mix of devils and skeletons became ever-present images on the remarkable postcards of Halloween.

Three cats, $8.00 – 10.00.

Child, jack-o-lantern, $22.00 – 28.00.

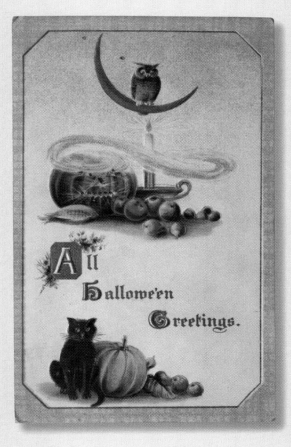

Owl, cat, posted 1911, $8.00 – 10.00.

Youngster, carving, Clapsaddle,
$35.00 – 40.00.

Woman, candle, $18.00 – 22.00.

Cat, rat, $18.00 – 22.00.

Carving scene, Clapsaddle, $35.00 – 40.00.

Scared theme, posted 1916, $30.00 – 35.00.

Smiling child, Brundage, $45.00 – 55.00.

Children's party, Brundage, $45.00 – 55.00.

Birds, ghost, $15.00 – 18.00.

Girl, alarm clock, $35.00 – 40.00.

Black cat, Clapsaddle, $45.00 – 55.00.

Happy Halloween, 1915, $15.00 – 18.00.

Clown costume, $35.00 – 38.00.

Woman, mirror, posted 1912,
$12.00 – 15.00.

Witch costume, $25.00 – 30.00.

Child, dog, Clapsaddle, $35.00 – 45.00.

Running Pumpkin, $25.00 – 30.00.

Howling Halloween, $25.00 – 35.00.

Thanksgiving

As holidays go, Thanksgiving is uniquely American. Certainly other countries of the world have celebrated their blessings and their harvest for thousands of years. But only the made-in-USA version sprang from the idea of feasts among the Native Americans and Pilgrims during the days of Plymouth Rock.

The American holiday of Thanksgiving has always been linked to the harvest of crops as the growing seasons fade finally to winter. The Indian summer is over, fruits and vegetables are stored away, and families might be drawn to the warmth of the fireplace and dream of a magnificent meal.

Lasso, turkey, copyright 1906, $8.00 – 10.00.

Historians assure us that letters written by the Pilgrims to friends and relatives in England and in personal diaries, document that the first American Thanksgiving observance took place in 1621. However most of those same historians conclude that the post-harvest celebration did not come to be a regular event until at least 1630. Thanksgiving was already popular in New England when in 1789 George Washington proclaimed a day of thanksgiving to commemorate the successful launching of the new national government under the United States Constitution. From that time forward Thanksgiving always included at least a twinge of patriotism, a theme which would sometimes be included on holiday postcards celebrating that occasion. Some 70 years later at the time of the Civil War, the popularity of the holiday had spread from New England to include much of the rest of the country. In 1863 President Abraham Lincoln called for a national day of thanksgiving in response to victories of the Union army at Vicksburg and at Gettysburg. Lincoln's proclamation designated the last Thursday of November be known as Thanksgiving Day. The proclamation however did not have the full force of law and instead left the observance pretty much up to individual states.

By the early 1900s, as the romance of holiday greeting postcards came into full flower, Thanksgiving was generally viewed throughout the United States as a very special event. Thanksgiving postcards often featured American flags, family gatherings, a well-laden table, and the now very traditional turkey in somber or in humorous regard. Some of the cards depicted a more or less contemporary observance of the holiday, either the preparation of a major meal or the consumption of a major meal. Other postcards presented more of an historical view with Pilgrims richly costumed.

Regardless of the time period on the postcard's scene, corn of some type was almost shown as often as the turkey. One corn-related legend has it that Indians hung three ears of corn and a gourd outside of the teepee in symbolism. The corn fed the birds but it also had the higher purpose of giving thanks for the proper weather for growing crops and for the endurance needed to tend the crops. Among early settlers the last sheaf of the harvest crop, be it corn or other grain, was put aside for the making of a doll. The corn doll may be called harvest mother, or with other grains, rye woman or barley lady. At any rate the grain, be it an ear or a bushel, remained a strong symbol of Thanksgiving early in the twentieth century.

Noted postcard artists who contributed Thanksgiving renderings included Ellen Clapsaddle, Frances Brundage, Bernardt Wall (Wall), and H.B. Griggs (H.B.G.). One of the most unusual Thanksgiving holiday postcard illustrations by Griggs involved various nightmare figures apparently suggesting indigestion as the result of a major meal. A message on the reverse of one of these cards in 1911 said, "Fatty has ate too much Thanksgiving Dinner. You must not do the same."

Interestingly when the great Thanksgiving turkey was not illustrated as dinner on the holiday postcard, it may be seen pulling a sort of chariot-ride for children or pulling a sort of cart filled with harvest goods. Notable greeting card publishers of that era, as they were with many other holiday postcards at the time, included Tuck and Sons, International Art Company, and John Winsch.

In terms of holiday greetings, the golden days of the postcard were the grandest for Thanksgiving. When folded greeting cards came along in the 1920s, the public was simply not interested in giving Thanksgiving the "paper" status it had once held. It remained a major American holiday but one almost entirely void of printed greetings.

Controversy came to the Thanksgiving holiday in 1938 when President Franklin Roosevelt broke precedent and proclaimed November 23 as Thanksgiving Day. At that time of economic depression it was believed that the "revised" date would give merchants a longer Christmas shopping season and thus encourage what little consumer spending was yet available. FDR's proclamation aroused considerable debate in America's heartland, and many state governors steadfastly refused to recognize the Roosevelt revision. Finally in 1941 the U.S. Congress moved to establish the Lincolnesque fourth Thursday in November as the legal date of the Thanksgiving holiday.

In the grand scope of holiday greetings, Thanksgiving did not thrive too long in the twentieth century. While postcards reigned, the holiday was well represented by leading artists and publishers of that time. Briefly from the early 1900s to the dawn of the 1920s, they rivaled Easter, Valentine's Day, and even Christmas in volume. However their glory days were lost with the beginnings of the folded greeting card.

Fireplace, International Art, posted 1907, $3.00 – 4.00.

Turkey pair, International Art, posted 1908, $4.00 – 5.00.

Pilgrim woman, posted 1909, $5.00 – 7.00.

Turkey, Clapsaddle, $6.00 – 8.00.

Pilgrim landing, $4.00 – 6.00.

Squirrel, pine cones, posted 1908, $3.00 – 4.00.

Autumn leaf, turkey, $3.00 – 4.00.

Wild turkey, copyright 1908, $3.00 – 4.00.

Single turkey, copyright 1908, $3.00 – 4.00.

Woman, turkeys, Tuck, $4.00 – 5.00.

Children, turkey, posted 1909, $5.00 – 6.00.

Fruits, $2.00 – 3.00.

Turkey pair, fruits, $2.00 – 3.00.

Costumed turkey, $10.00 – 12.00.

Autumn scene, posted 1910, $3.00 – 4.00.

Wine glass, posted 1910, $3.00 – 4.00.

**Autumn leaves, Clapsaddle,
$4.00 – 5.00.**

**Turkey and child, posted
1909, $5.00 – 6.00.**

American Beauty, $3.00 – 4.00.

Thanksgiving Greetings, $4.00 – 5.00.

Patriotic theme, $6.00 – 8.00.

Souvenir spoon, $3.00 – 4.00.

Turkey, pasture, $4.00 – 5.00.

Turkey, woodland scene, $5.00 – 6.00.

Turkey in pumpkin, $4.00 – 5.00.

Fall leaves, turkey, $5.00 – 6.00.

Sailing ship, posted 1911, $5.00 – 7.00.

Rich blessings, $2.00 – 3.00.

Nightmare, H.B. Griggs,
$15.00 – 20.00.

Preparing meal,
$5.00 – 6.00.

Flowers, turkey, $4.00 – 5.00.

Turkey, farm scene, $6.00 – 8.00.

Maiden, turkey, copyright 1911,
$8.00 – 10.00.

Turkey pulls cart, $6.00 – 8.00.

Feast, posted 1911, $3.00 – 4.00.

Child, turkey, H.B. Griggs, $10.00 – 12.00.

Girl and cart, $6.00 – 8.00.

Thanksgiving wish,
$4.00 – 5.00.

Burns poem, $4.00 – 5.00.

Turkey and chariot,
$6.00 – 8.00.

Boy with apple, $5.00 – 6.00.

Home, turkey, $3.00 – 4.00.

Children, turkey pull, H.B. Griggs, $8.00 – 10.00.

Turkey, grapevine, $3.00 – 4.00.

Autumn splendor, $2.00 – 3.00.

Turkey, pine cones, $3.00 – 4.00.

Flower vase, turkey, $4.00 – 5.00.

Girl and turkey, $8.00 – 10.00.

Corn, corn popper, $2.00 – 3.00.

*Turkey, patriotic symbol,
$5.00 – 6.00.*

Chef and turkey, $4.00 – 6.00.

Turkey, harvest, $5.00 – 6.00.

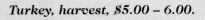

Lake scene, $2.00 – 3.00.

Intricate design, $3.00 – 4.00.

Cordial Greetings, $2.00 – 3.00.

Girl feeds turkey, $6.00 – 8.00.

With Thanksgiving, $2.00 – 3.00.

Pilgrims, cow, $4.00 – 5.00.

Lamp lights table,
$5.00 – 6.00.

Pilgrim children, posted
1915, $6.00 – 8.00.

Flowers, turkey, $2.00 – 3.00.

Happy Thanksgiving, $3.00 – 4.00.

Feeding turkey, $5.00 – 6.00.

Joyful Thanksgiving, $4.00 – 5.00.

Best Wishes, $4.00 – 5.00.

Bright Thanksgiving, $3.00 – 4.00.

Preparing pumpkin, $4.00 – 5.00.

Greetings, copyright 1917,
$6.00 – 8.00.

Little girl, turkey,
$6.00 – 8.00.

Girl, turkey cart,
$12.00 – 18.00.

Carving turkey, $6.00 – 8.00.

When harvest comes, $2.00 – 3.00.

*Thanksgiving wish, Clapsaddle,
$18.00 – 22.00.*

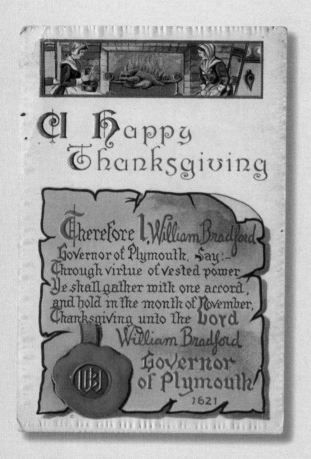

Happy Thanksgiving, $5.00 – 6.00.

Farm scene, $4.00 – 5.00.

Turkey, vines, $4.00 – 5.00.

Child with basket, $6.00 – 7.00.

Cordial greetings, $3.00 – 4.00.

Turkey, U.S. flag, $10.00 – 12.00.

Farm bushels, $4.00 – 5.00.

Bountiful Thanksgiving,
$2.00 – 3.00.

Family gathering, $5.00 – 6.00.

Turkey, corn, $4.00 – 5.00.

Children, basket, $5.00 – 6.00.

Girl atop pumpkin, $4.00 – 5.00.

Pilgrim woman, $4.00 – 5.00.

Harvest moon, $2.00 – 3.00.

Child, pumpkin, $2.00 – 3.00.

Child and turkey, $5.00 – 6.00.

Farm field, $3.00 – 4.00.

Turkey on fence, $4.00 – 5.00.

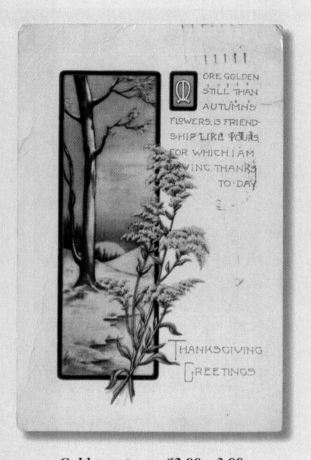

ORE GOLDEN
STILL THAN
AUTUMN'S
FLOWERS, IS FRIEND-
SHIP LIKE YOURS
FOR WHICH I AM
GIVING THANKS
TO-DAY

THANKSGIVING
GREETINGS

Golden autumn, $2.00 – 3.00.

THANKSGIVING

MAY ALL YOUR DAYS BE THANKFUL
AND MAY YOUR WHOLE LIFE BE
RICH AS THE GOLDEN HARVEST
THAT AT TURKEY-TIME WE SEE

Farmer boy, turkey, $15.00 – 18.00.

THANKSGIVING
GREETINGS

Child on fence, $12.00 – 14.00.

Harvest scene, $5.00 – 6.00.

Corn, church, $4.00 – 5.00.

Thanksgiving wish, $4.00 – 5.00.

Turkey in tree, $2.00. – 3.00.

Thanksgiving cheer, $10.00 – 12.00.

Christmas — Traditional

Christmas undoubtedly had more impact on the early twentieth century business of holiday greeting postcards than any other holiday.

In terms of numbers there were probably more Christmas greeting postcards published during the height of their popularity than all others combined. They were lavishly illustrated with angels, animals, birds, children, church views, flowers (especially the richly red poinsettia), holly, manger scenes, sleds, snow scenes, and Christmas trees. From the first years of the 1900s through the 1920s they were published by the hundreds of thousands.

Christmas postcards arrived at just the time when Americans were displaying a widespread interest in exchanging the printed word of holiday greetings. Americans had been sending out Christmas greetings at a fairly brisk pace in the 1880s but as such greetings required envelopes, the practice was expensive and the mail service of the nineteenth century was relatively slow and undependable. Still by the 1890s the demand for Christmas greeting cards had increased to the point where European printers, especially those in Germany, began to see the overwhelming potential of the American market. In England the master of such greeting cards was the Raphael Tuck Company which also had its eye on the marketing potential of the United States.

Early in the 1900s this status report appeared in one leading American publication:

The general custom of sending Christmas cards to friends is practiced in Great Britain and on the continent. The members of the British royal family have cards especially designed for them by Raphael Tuck and Sons.

Despite the great possibilities, the very earliest of the Christmas greeting postcards were not that impressive. Basically local and regional merchants used standard view postcards and simply stamped or overprinted such phrases as best Christmas wishes or compliments of the season. Often the scene on the postcard was not even illustrative of the winter season much less of any yuletide images. Eventually however there was a merger between the quality postcard publishers and the public's demand for graphic but yet not too expensive Christmas greetings.

In *The Christmas Book* written by Jane Stewart in 1908 the author pointed out the national trend:

The Christmas card has been given the postal card form by placing the outline for the address and the postage stamp on its back. In this way it has become even more firmly established in the hearts of the people, and given even wider extension. Only the less expensive cards can be sent this way, the price not usually exceeding five cents.

Stewart then added this afterthought:

Christmas cards, whether sent as postcards or enclosed like letters, are responsible for much of the universal goodwill and happiness of Christmas Day.

Holly, script, posted 1905, $3.00 – 4.00.

As happy as the Christmas greeting postcards may have been at that time, very, very few bore any religious tone. Glad tidings more often featured children or adults celebrating the holiday, mistletoe draped upon a basket or framed on a pastoral view, or perhaps a warm fireplace with or without Christmas stockings. But there were relatively small numbers of postcards depicting the Christ child, the Virgin Mary, or a setting in Bethlehem. Decades later, in 1970, one writer commented on this same situation. C.W. Hill observed in the book, *Discovering Picture Post Cards:*

"Complaints are frequently heard that the designs of many modern Christmas cards (1970) are too secular, conveying little or nothing of the religious significance of the Christian festival. A similar criticism might well be directed against some of the picture postcards used for sending Christmas greetings early in the twentieth century." Hill offered no real explanation for the lack of religious oriented postcards in the 1900s, but his observance was well founded.

Holly, landscape. posted 1905 $2.00 – 3.00.

Whatever the situation there is no doubt that the people of that period were quite enthusiastic about the Christmas holiday. Some of the hand-written messages on the backs of the cards offer some otherwise rare looks into the thoughts of that generation of Americans as they observed the event. A 1911 card depicted holly and the sunrise. On the reverse the sender wrote, "I got a ring for Xmas. You ought to have been here and went to the Xmas tree." Another dated 1910 with bluebirds and bells was apparently sent by a neighbor, "Stanley, may you live to see many a merry Christmas and no mumps, your neighbor E.C."

Postcard publishers made every effort to make their Christmas greeting postcards as colorful and as graphic as possible. Some even used glitter to highlight the holiday images. The glitter or sparkle was actually tiny grains of metal sprinkled on the pictures.

"Women's dresses, the outlines of buildings in night scenes, and the petals of flowers," were some of the images to which glitter was added according to Hill. "Unfortunately such decorations were not so attractive to mail carriers, who complained that the gains of metal made their hands sore."

For a time postal officials in the United States and England fought the glitter decorated Christmas postcards, and in some cases ruled that the glitter came under the heading of attachments to a basic postcard. If an attachment was made to the greeting postcard the cost of mailing it would double from one cent to two cents. Briefly some postcard publishers experimented with putting the highly decorated cards in covers for mailing. Ultimately however the problem was solved with improvements in printing which allowed postcard publishers to use brilliant dashes of various colored inks upon their Christmas images.

In England, Raphael Tuck and Sons lived up to their reputation of being the publishers for royalty by issuing very distinguished holiday greeting postcards for the Christmas season. In America the work of Ellen Clapsaddle, among others, continued to deliver its endearing appeal on Christmas greeting postcards.

Interestingly during the true glory days of the Christmas postcard, mailing early for the holidays apparently did not have the meaning it currently holds in the twenty-first century. A study of postmarks of the early Christmas postcards reveals that many were mailed just days before the holiday or actually on Christmas eve and yet, somehow, the post office managed to deliver them on Christmas morning.

By the 1920s people in the United States were gradually advancing toward the use of folded Christmas cards which involved an envelope and a bit more postage. Still postcard publishers produced some excellent examples of Christmas greetings which are among those highly collectible today.

Sled, Clapsaddle, $6.00 – 8.00.

Holly, home, $2.00 – 3.00.

Poinsettia flowers,
$3.00 – 4.00.

Family scene, posted 1906,
$8.00 – 10.00.

House in winter, $2.00 – 3.00.

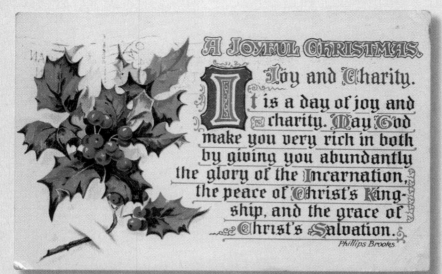

Brooks poem, $2.00 – 3.00.

Stylish woman, $3.00 – 5.00.

Flower, $2.00 – 3.00.

Angel with flowers, $6.00 – 9.00.

Good luck, posted 1907, $2.00 – 3.00.

Happy Christmas, $2.00 – 3.00.

Church, bird, posted 1907, $3.00 – 4.00.

Pair of birds, $3.00 – 4.00.

Birds on branch, $2.00 – 3.00.

Children reading, Tuck, $8.00 – 10.00.

Children, snowman, $6.00 – 8.00.

Child, posted 1908, $5.00 – 6.00.

Child's face, Tuck, $4.00 – 5.00.

Two girls, posted 1908, $5.00 – 6.00.

Hooded child, $3.00 – 4.00.

Costumed children, posted 1908,
$5.00 – 7.00.

Bells, angels, posted 1909, $4.00 – 5.00.

Loving angels, posted 1909,
$6.00 – 8.00.

From Nineveh, $3.00 – 4.00.

Kiss, patriotic, posted 1909, $10.00 – 12.00.

Asian theme, posted 1909, $6.00 – 8.00.

Angel, deer, posted 1909, $4.00 – 5.00.

Children skating, $12.00 – 15.00.

Girl, doll, posted 1909, $6.00 – 8.00.

Children sledding, damaged, $5.00 – 6.00.

Winter scene, $2.00 – 3.00.

Portrait, copyright 1907
National Art, $5.00 – 6.00.

Angel, $6.00 – 8.00.

Church scene, posted 1909, $4.00 – 5.00.

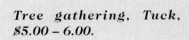

Tree gathering, Tuck, $5.00 – 6.00.

Horseshoe, holly, $2.00 – 3.00.

Loving Christmas, $2.00 – 3.00.

Embossed angel, $6.00 – 7.00.

Sledding, $6.00 – 8.00.

Wishing you, $3.00 – 4.00.

Reindeer, forest, $4.00 – 5.00.

Harp, posted 1909, $3.00 – 4.00.

Candles, holly, $2.00 – 3.00.

Snow covered tree, $2.00 – 3.00.

Little girl, $6.00 – 8.00.

Christ, tree, $6.00 – 8.00.

Telegram, $3.00 – 4.00.

Snow scene, $3.00 – 4.00.

Horses, $5.00 – 6.00.

House, rabbit, $2.00 – 3.00.

Snowy road, $2.00 – 3.00.

Bell, posted 1909, $2.00 – 3.00.

House, holly, $2.00 – 3.00.

Stained glass, posted 1911, $6.00 – 7.00.

Kind thoughts, $2.00 – 3.00.

Bird, church, $2.00 – 3.00.

Bell, snow scene, $3.00 – 4.00.

Cat, vase, $5.00 – 7.00.

Bells, ribbon, $3.00 – 4.00.

Clock, $4.00 – 5.00.

Snow scene, $2.00 – 3.00.

Happy Christmas, $2.00 – 3.00.

Christ child, $5.00 – 6.00.

Church, posted 1911, $5.00 – 6.00.

Cordial Christmas, $2.00 – 3.00.

Happy   Memories, $2.00 – 3.00.

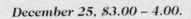

December 25, $3.00 – 4.00.

Puppy dogs, $5.00 – 6.00.

All happiness, $2.00 – 3.00.

Box of holly, $2.00 – 3.00.

Season's greeting, $5.00 – 6.00.

Kind and true, $2.00 – 3.00.

Good wishes, $5.00 – 6.00.

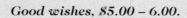

Bells, $2.00 – 3.00.

Holly, church, $3.00 – 4.00.

Birds, bells, $2.00 – 3.00.

Volumes, $3.00 – 4.00.

Glad tidings, $3.00 – 4.00.

Christmas day, posted 1911, $2.00 – 3.00.

Happy bells, $2.00 – 3.00.

I THINK OF YOU THE SEASONS THROUGH—
AND SO IT'S HARDLY QUEER,
THAT AT THE STROKE OF TWELVE I RISE,
AND WISH YOU NEW YEAR CHEER.

Hardly queer, Tuck, $6.00 – 8.00.

With Best Wishes for a Merry Christmas

Woman, flowers, $3.00 – 5.00.

Christmas song, $2.00 – 3.00.

A Happy Christmas Song

Hearty wishes, posted 1911, $3.00 – 4.00.

Religious, $5.00 – 6.00.

Hearty greetings, $3.00 – 4.00.

Christ child, $6.00 – 8.00.

Flowers, $2.00 – 3.00.

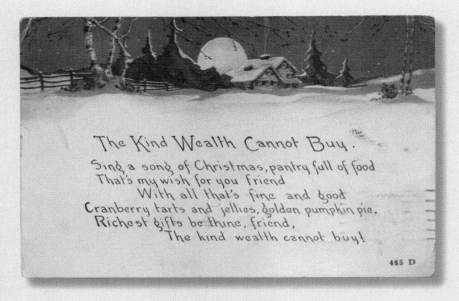

The Kind Wealth Cannot Buy.

Sing a song of Christmas, pantry full of food
That's my wish for you friend
With all that's fine and good
Cranberry tarts and jellies, golden pumpkin pie,
Richest gifts be thine, friend,
The kind wealth cannot buy!

485 D

Wealth Cannot Buy, $3.00 – 4.00.

Right happy, $3.00 – 4.00.

Doves, bells, $2.00 – 3.00.

Girl in dress, posted 1911, $6.00 – 7.00.

Wishbone, $7.00 – 8.00.

Mary and child, $6.00 – 8.00.

Horseshoe, house, $3.00 – 4.00.

Small angel, posted 1911, $6.00 – 8.00.

Church scene, $5.00 – 6.00.

Woman with bonnet, $4.00 – 5.00.

Child, Christmas tree, $6.00 – 7.00.

Child, toys, $8.00 – 9.00.

Angel reads book, $5.00 – 6.00.

Mother, Christ child, $5.00 – 6.00.

Christmas, gold trimmed, $3.00 – 4.00.

Joyous Christmastide, $3.00 – 4.00.

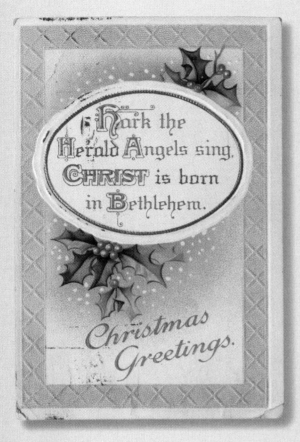

*Hark the Herald Angels sing, posted 1911,
$2.00 – 3.00.*

*Merry Christmas, copyright 1912,
$3.00 – 4.00.*

Three angels, $3.00 – 4.00.

Church scene, $4.00 – 5.00.

*A Greeting, Winsch 1912,
$3.00 – 4.00.*

*Christmas flowers, posted
1912, $4.00 – 5.00.*

Children decorate tree, $8.00 – 10.00.

Church, copyright 1912, $4.00 – 5.00.

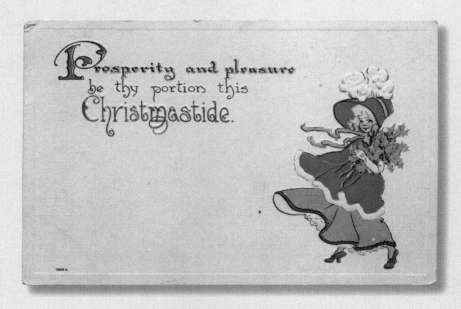

Prosperity, pleasure, $4.00 – 5.00.

Manger scene, $4.00 – 5.00.

Joyful Christmas, $2.00 – 3.00.

Blue jay, $3.00 – 4.00.

Best wishes, posted 1912,
$2.00 – 3.00.

Boxed gift image, posted
1912, $4.00 – 5.00.

Four kittens, $5.00 – 6.00.

Street scene, posted 1913, $3.00 – 4.00.

Bells chime, $4.00 – 5.00.

Auto travel, $4.00 – 5.00.

Child and dog, $8.00 – 10.00.

Child, telephone, posted 1913,
$10.00 – 11.00.

Cat, $4.00 – 5.00.

Sheep, shepherd, $3.00 – 4.00.

Children, Santa in sky, $6.00 – 8.00.

Snow-covered house, $2.00 – 3.00.

Basket, holly, $3.00 – 4.00.

Religious, $3.00 – 4.00.

Child makes list,
$6.00 – 8.00.

Girl and cat, dated 1914,
$10.00 – 12.00.

Children, tree,
$8.00 – 10.00.

Children, sled, posted 1915,
$6.00 – 8.00.

Stream, bridge, $3.00 – 4.00.

Cheery Christmas!

We're gathered round the fireplace
Come share it with us, we entreat;
If we could see your smiling face
Our Christmas then would be complete.

Cheery fireplace, $3.00 – 5.00.

Snow-covered church, $6.00 – 8.00.

Child and holly, $6.00 – 8.00.

Children in sled, posted 1914,
$16.00 – 18.00.

Cat in basket, $5.00 – 6.00.

**Children with socks,
$10.00 – 12.00.**

**Child at fireplace,
$8.00 – 10.00.**

**Child and gifts, posted
1917, $18.00 – 22.00.**

Snowball fight, $8.00 – 10.00.

Remembrance, posted 1917, $2.00 – 3.00.

California Christmas, posted 1917, $6.00 – 8.00.

Girl and skates, $8.00 – 10.00.

Signpost, $2.00 – 3.00.

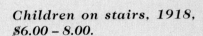

Children on stairs, 1918,
$6.00 – 8.00.

When stars shine down
    on Christmas night;
And candles, too, are brightly
    burning on your tree.
Amid your pleasures
        and your fun,
Your thoughts will travel,
    and you'll surely think of me
And I shall think of you as well
Looking ahead to
    happy meetings yet to be.

Christmas tree, posted 1918, $5.00 – 6.00.

Christmas, John Winsch, $3.00 – 4.00.

A MERRY CHRISTMAS

A Very Happy Christmas

The bird is blithely singing, to bring happiness to you.

Bluebird, posted 1918, $3.00 – 4.00.

Young woman, posted 1918, $6.00 – 8.00.

Girl, Clapsaddle, $16.00 – 18.00.

Good Wishes, $3.00 – 5.00.

Happy Xmas, posted 1919, $3.00 – 4.00.

American flags, $6.00 – 8.00.

Spinning wheel, $2.00 – 3.00.

Girl, winter gear, $8.00 – 10.00.

Snowy Christmas, $4.00 – 5.00.

From California, 1920, $6.00 – 8.00.

Child eating, posted 1922, $5.00 – 6.00.

Tree, fireplace, $4.00 – 5.00.

Stagecoach, posted 1922, $3.00 – 5.00.

Sled scene, $2.00 – 3.00.

MAY EVERY GOOD FORTUNE BE YOURS TODAY

AND MEMORIES OF CHRISTMAS ABIDE FOR AYE.

Greetings of the
Season
The same good hearty wishes I'm sending
as of old. May Christmas come to you
and yours with blessings manifold.

Greetings of Season, 1922,
$2.00 – 3.00.

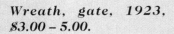

Wreath, gate, 1923,
$3.00 – 5.00.

A CHRISTMAS GREETING

Here comes a big hearty wish for a Merry Christmas.

Package delivery, 1922, $5.00 – 6.00.

May all the Christmas Joys be Yours

Child, gift, 1923, $6.00 – 8.00.

A Happy Christmas!

Decorated tree, 1923, $6.00 – 8.00.

Snow scene, $2.00 – 3.00.

Merrie Christmas, $3.00 – 5.00.

Cordial Greetings,
$3.00 – 5.00.

Children and toys, 1923, $8.00 – 10.00.

Angel on bell, $6.00 – 8.00.

Christmas angel, $6.00 – 8.00.

*Village scene,
$3.00 – 4.00.*

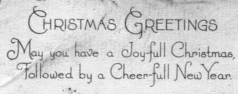

*Children, instruments,
$4.00 – 5.00.*

*Girl and doll, posted 1924,
$8.00 – 10.00.*

Child, snow, $3.00 – 4.00.

Manger site, posted 1924, $5.00 – 6.00.

Girl and gifts, posted 1925, $8.00 – 10.00.

Hanging stockings, posted 1926,
$8.00 – 10.00.

Christmastide, $5.00 – 6.00.

Candle, house, $2.00 – 3.00.

May Christmas bring you peace and plenty
And the New Year be full of pleasantness.

To Grandma
From Dorothy A.

**Religious, 1927,
$3.00 – 5.00.**

The Season's Best Wishes!

As happy as the shepherds
When they heard the angel say:
"To you is born at Bethlehem
A Savior on this day."
So happy may you also be
As once again you hear
The Christmas tidings of good-will,
And grace, and peace, and cheer!

"Unto you is born this day a Savior." Luke 2,11.

Bethlehem angel, $3.00 – 5.00.

Best Wishes

May the Christmas Star
which led the Wise Men
long ago, guide you,
As then it guided them
to joy on earth,
peace to all men.

Wise Men, $3.00 – 5.00.

Hello folks, posted 1930, $10.00 – 12.00.

Radio Broadcast, $3.00 – 5.00.

Christmas — Santa Claus

Postcards featuring Santa Claus represent a class by themselves when it comes to holiday greeting postcards. Early in the twentieth century postcards probably did more than any other print medium to establish the jolly elf firmly in the American mindset.

On greeting postcards Santa could be found in a long green robe or wearing a modern Americanized red suit. Santa could be puffing upon his pipe or unloading toys from his sack. For nearly two decades Santa was everywhere on postcards in just about every type of costume and setting. While traditional Christmas postcards seemed to go in one direction, the image of Santa Claus seemed to evolve in another direction. Today those varying yet classic conceptions of Santa are among the most collectible of all holiday postcards.

Certainly the idea and even the illustration of Santa was around long before the American postcard. *Knickerbocker's History of New York* in 1809 made over two dozen references to Sin-

Santa inset, posted 1908, $5.00 – 7.00.

terklass and St. Nicholas. He was described as wearing a low, broad-brimmed hat and Flemish trunk-hose. Moreover he rode a flying wagon and delivered presents down the chimney to waiting children. The book was quite popular at the time and undoubtedly did much to further some sort of Santa image in the minds of all its readers. In 1821, a book called *The Children's Friend* used a lithographed illustration to depict a whiskered elf-like figure with a tall brown hat and green jacket. His name in the book was Santeclaus. The very next year, Episcopal clergyman Clement Moore wrote the now famous poem, *A Visit from St. Nicholas*. The account, which is currently referred to as *The Night Before Christmas*, has Santa as a "jolly old elf" who was "chubby and plump" and dressed in fur. Instead of the earlier flying wagon, he rode in a sleigh pulled by reindeer. Moore's poem was not published in book form until 1837. It was illustrated by United States Military Academy professor Robert Weir. As could be expected Weir's Santa was of course both plump and jolly. He wore a red cape with white fur, and carried a bag of presents on his back.

Political cartoonist Thomas Nast began creating illustrations of Santa during the 1860s both for *Harper's Weekly* and for a children's book which was first published in 1863. Nast's version often wore a long red robe trimmed in fur. Like earlier American versions Nast's Santa remained jolly and kindly, unlike an earlier sterner and humorless figure popular in Germany.

During the 1870s Britain's notable and ambitious Raphael Tuck began offering a full line of Christmas greetings. By the following decade much of the budding British and American market in Christmas greeting cards had given away to somewhat less expensive cards being printed in Germany. Shortly before the dawn of the twentieth century, a determined Tuck lead efforts in England to provide reduced postal rates for privately printed postcards. Adoption of the same basic idea in the United States lead to a golden age of lavishly printed Christmas and other striking greeting postcards. (Tuck's elaborate postcards directed at the American market are noted frequently in this volume.)

Eventually Raphael Tuck and Sons would produce a number of specialized Santa Claus post-cards for distribution mostly in the United States. Tuck and other publishers did not restrict themselves to any particular version of Santa. Generally from 1904 to 1918 Santa could be found in blue, green, gold, brown, and white cloth as well as the now standard red suit. Sometimes the clothing was robe-like, at other times it was clearly a suit consisting of a jacket and separate pants. Usually the jacket and pants were of the same color, but occasionally a stylish Santa wore a red jacket with contrasting blue pants.

The variations were in fact endless. Santa might be wearing a purple hat while surrounded by toys. A more regal Santa might be wearing a gold hat decked with pine cones. On other postcards he might have no hat at all. Santa could often be found, like the Moore poem, smoking a pipe. But he might also be found smoking a cigar or sipping a glass of champagne. Santa could be found peering into a window, standing in front of the fireplace, or inspecting his workshop records. And Santa's transportation, as shown on the early holiday postcards, could vary considerably too. He might be trudging along on foot, driving an automobile, gliding in a sleigh, or riding on a horse-drawn sled. Likewise he could be handing out a pair of ice skates or offering up gifts from an entire bag filled with toys. Sometimes Santa even brought a decorated Christmas tree along with him.

Beyond the very striking but basic Santa postcards, there were also elaborate versions such as hold-to-light cards, glitter decorated cards (see Christmas – Traditional), die-cut mechanical cards where a dial was turned to make Santa appear from a winter scene, and installment cards providing individual sections that formed a full figure when eventually put together. Even more scarce are those postcards showing children dressed as Santa, a female Santa, or a black Santa. Perhaps the rarest were those that mixed the holiday season with patriotism and depicted Uncle Sam in the role of Santa Claus.

Thousands of Santa postcards were rendered by unknown and unheralded artists, but there was also the work of such notables as Frances Brundage and Ellen Clapsaddle. More traditional artists such as Raphael Kirchner and cartoonist Richard Felton Outcault were also known to have illustrated the fabled figure on postcards of the early twentieth century. Outcault used his legendary Buster Brown figure and Santa for a series of advertising postcards used by Bloomingdale's department store in New York City. Santa was frequently used on regular and commercial postcards of the later decades but they were often lacking in the variety and graphic splendor of years prior to 1930.

Fond greetings, posted 1908, $5.00 – 6.00.

Santa, toys, tree, $18.00 – 25.00.

Child, Santa mask, $8.00 – 10.00.

Santa rings bells, posted 1909,
$6.00 – 8.00.

Embossed Santa, posted 1909, $5.00 – 6.00.

Santa with tree, posted 1910, $6.00 – 8.00.

Santa outside, posted 1909, $5.00 – 6.00.

Santa at desk, $18.00 – 20.00.

Brother's Delight, posted 1911, $8.00 – 10.00.

Wearing holly, $6.00 – 8.00.

Blue outfit, posted 1911, $6.00 – 8.00.

Busy Santa, letters, $8.00 – 10.00.

Papa's Delight, $8.00 – 10.00.

**Smoking cigar, posted 1911,
$18.00 – 22.00.**

Santa in sleigh, $6.00 – 8.00.

**Hooded Santa, children,
$6.00 – 8.00.**

Santa behind clock, posted 1911,
$8.00 – 10.00.

Odd-colored robe, staff, $22.00 – 26.00.

Gold glitter, $20.00 – 22.00.

Purple hat, toys, $28.00 – 34.00.

Santa, holly, $10.00 – 12.00.

Green outfit, $25.00 – 30.00.

Smiling Santa, creasing, $5.00 – 7.00.

Santa and deer, damage, $3.00 – 5.00.

Sleeping children, $18.00 – 20.00.

Inset Santa, $5.00 – 6.00.

Santa and book, posted 1913, $6.00 – 8.00.

Santa and candle, posted 1916, $6.00 – 8.00.

Little girl, $8.00 – 10.00.

Best wishes, posted 1916, $5.00 – 6.00.

Christmas joys, $5.00 – 6.00.

Brown hat, $5.00 – 6.00.

Child at window, $6.00 – 7.00.

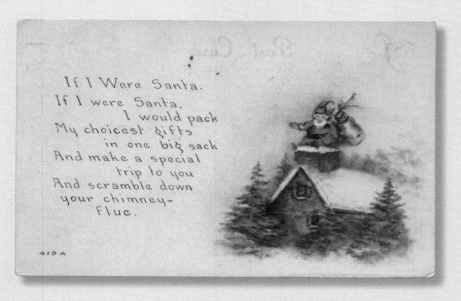

Santa poem, posted 1917, $4.00 – 5.00.

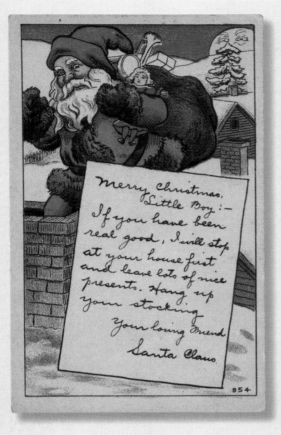

Santa letter, $8.00 – 9.00.

Santa wishes, posted 1919, $3.00 – 5.00.

Here I come, posted 1921, $6.00 – 8.00.

Merry one, posted 1921, $5.00 – 6.00.

Laughing Santa, $5.00 – 6.00.

Christmas cheer, $6.00 – 7.00.

I'm hoping, posted 1923,
$4.00 – 5.00.

Going down, $6.00 – 8.00.

Jolly as holly, posted 1923,
$5.00 – 6.00.

Santa and sleigh, 1922, $6.00 – 8.00.

Boy and girl, $8.00 – 10.00.

Merry Christmas, $4.00 – 5.00.

Filling stockings, posted 1926,
$6.00 – 8.00.

Red suit, posted 1930, $6.00 – 8.00.

Jolly Christmas, posted 1928, $4.00 – 5.00.

Santa with sign, $4.00 – 5.00.

Santa in sky, posted 1931, $6.00 – 8.00.

Special Holidays

It is not that special holidays were not celebrated well before the arrival of postcards, they were. It is just that it would have been rare to have sent or received a store bought greetings card noting a birthday, anniversary, baby's arrival, graduation, or simply just "best wishes."

As has been previously noted there were commercially printed Christmas greeting cards and Valentine's Day greeting cards during the nineteenth century. But any other holiday, much less a personal occasion, was not likely to be committed to formal printing. All that changed dramatically with the establishment of the greetings postcard.

Even best wishes, birthdays, and such could now be celebrated with brightly printed and easy-to-mail postcards. The more graphic and appealing the better. Right along with the major holidays, special holiday cards were given the same high-quality printing process. Sometimes the elaborate treatment including gold gilding, glitter, or shiny embossing.

At the height of the postcard greeting mania, birthday and best wishes cards were available throughout America in nearly every retail store, large and small. In fact some stores actually specialized in postcards themselves with hundreds and hundreds of gleaming selections. During that era it was probably much easier (and cheaper) for the average shopper to find an appropriate greeting card than to find an appropriate gift.

Perhaps best of all the chromolithographed treasures could be mailed anywhere in the United States for a mere one cent. The vast majority of the cards were lavishly illustrated by accomplished printers in Germany who dominated that aspect of the business until high tariffs made American printing more competitive. Like the major holidays, special holiday postcards were also sometimes illustrated by leading artists of the day including Ellen Clapsaddle, Rose O'Neill, Frances Brundage, H.B. Griggs, and others.

A gilded rose, an elf with golden wings, a dove amid a scene of flowers, and fashionably dressed women and children were all available to help express the fondest thought. The recipient would be thrilled, and more than likely be moved to save the colorful postcard as part of their collection. Almost everyone in America was entertained and romanced with the charm of greeting postcards. An exception was G.W. Green who wrote in the *Atlantic Monthly* magazine during the dawn of the postcard, that they were simply too readable by others.

My grudge against the postal card is the tendency to read, against your own will, postal cards not addressed to yourself. There is a fascination about the thing which is very like kleptomania.

Probably the writer had something in mind like the penciled message on a wedding congratulations postcard. Mailed around 1908, the reverse of the card read:

Accept the kindest wishes of a friend who greets you at your wedding hour. May guardian angels on your steps attend. My heaven its blessings on you shower.

With due regard for other points of view, the messages offer delightful insights from the common folk who felt so fondly about greetings on postcards.

Horseshoe, posted 1908, $3.00 – 4.00.

Fairy and rose, posted
1908, $4.00 – 5.00.

Hat, roses, posted 1910,
$3.00 – 4.00.

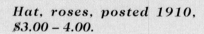

Dove, posted 1911,
$4.00 – 5.00.

Colonial woman, 1911, $3.00 – 4.00.

Stylish girls, posted 1911, $4.00 – 5.00.

Flowers, posted 1913, $3.00 – 4.00.

Bridge scene, $2.00 – 3.00.

Dog and basket, posted 1908, $4.00 – 5.00.

Automobile, $3.00 – 4.00.

Girls and dove, posted 1909, $3.00 – 4.00.

Telephone, $3.00 – 4.00.

Sailboat, posted 1909, $3.00 – 4.00.

Baby on scales, $5.00 – 6.00.

Young woman, posted 1910, $2.00 – 3.00.

Church scene, $2.00 – 3.00.

Girl with basket, $5.00 – 6.00.

Mailboy, posted 1910, $6.00 – 8.00.

Birds, posted 1911, $3.00 – 4.00.

Doves, dated 1914, $3.00 – 4.00.

Friend most true, $2.00 – 3.00.

Upon carriage, $4.00 – 5.00.

Bird delivery, posted 1918, $3.00 – 4.00.

Girl watering, 1922, $3.00 – 4.00.

Girl and bouquet, $2.00 – 3.00.

Good Luck, posted 1907, $2.00 – 3.00.

To Greet You, posted 1911, $3.00 – 4.00.

Wedding, dated 1909, $6.00 – 8.00.

New baby, $6.00 – 8.00.

Sweet flowers, posted 1913, $3.00 – 4.00.

Remembrance, posted 1911, $3.00 – 4.00.

Greetings, posted 1915, $3.00 – 4.00.

Remember me, gold gild, 1916,
$5.00 – 6.00.

Happy returns, Tuck, posted 1912, $6.00 – 8.00.

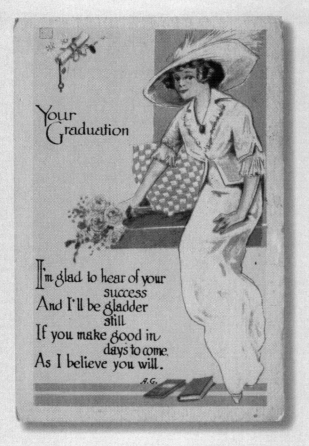

Your
Graduation

I'm glad to hear of your
success
And I'll be gladder
still
If you make good in
days to come,
As I believe you will.

A.G.

Your graduation, $5.00 – 6.00.

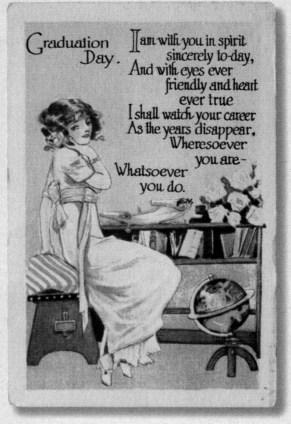

Graduation
Day.

I am with you in spirit
sincerely to-day,
And with eyes ever
friendly and heart
ever true
I shall watch your career
As the years disappear,
Wheresoever
you are -

Whatsoever
you do.

Graduation Day, $5.00 – 6.00.

A Loving Thought

Loving thought, posted 1914, $2.00 – 3.00.

Bibliography

Allen, Frederick Lewis. *Only Yesterday.* New York, New York: Harper & Brothers Publishers, 1931.

Auld, William M. *Christmas Traditions.* New York, New York: The Macmillan Company, 1931.

Denton, Clara. *New Years to Christmas in Holiday Land.* Chicago, Illinois: Albert Whitman & Co., 1928.

Hadfield, John. *The Christmas Companion.* New York, New York: J. M. Dent & Sons Ltd., 1941.

Reed, Robert. *Advertising Postcards.* Atglen, Pennsylvania: Schiffer Publishing, 2001.

——. *Paper Advertising Collectibles.* Norfork, Virginia: Antique Trader Books, 1998.

——. *Paper Collectibles.* Pennsylvania, Randor: Antique Trader Books, 1998.

McSpadden, J. Walker. *The Book of Holidays.* New York, New York: Thomas V. Crowell Company, 1917.

Schneider, Stuart. *Halloween in America.* Atglen, Pennsylvania: Schiffer Publishing, 1995.

Stewart, Jane A. *The Christmas Book.* Philadelphia, Pennsylvania: The Griffith & Rowland Press, 1908.

Whitmyer, Margaret & Kenn. *Christmas Collectibles, 2nd Edition.* Paducah, Kentucky: Collector Books, 1994.

Wirth, Fremont. *The Development of America.* Boston, Massachusetts: American Book Company, 1938.